Collins

Effective Meetings

IN 7 SIMPLE STEPS

Collins

HarperCollins Publishers
77-85 Fulham Palace Road
Hammersmith
London W6 8JB

First edition 2014
Reprint 10 9 8 7 6 5 4 3 2 1 0
© HarperCollins Publishers 2014
ISBN 978-0-00-750720-7
Collins® is a registered trademark of HarperCollins Publishers Limited
www.collinselt.com
A catalogue record for this book is available from the British Library
Typeset in India by Aptara
Printed and bound in Great Britain by Clays Ltd, St Ives plc

Illustrations by Scott Garrett

MIX
Paper from
responsible sources

FSC™ C007454
www.fsc.org

FSC™ is a non-profit international organisation established to promote the responsible management of the world's forests. Products carrying the FSC label are independently certified to assure consumers that they come from forests that are managed to meet the social, economic and ecological needs of present and future generations, and other controlled sources.

Find out more about HarperCollins and the environment at
www.harpercollins.co.uk/green

Contents

About the author

Barry Tomalin trains companies in international communication techniques and teaches International Communication and Management skills at the London Academy of Diplomacy, University of East Anglia. He has worked for the British Council and the BBC World Service and is the author of *Key Business Skills* (HarperCollins 2012). Barry has attended and run more meetings than he cares to remember, during which time he has made mistakes and learned how to get things right most of the time.

Step 1

ORGANISE PEOPLE, PLACES AND TIMES

'Did we make a decision in there?'
—US executive after a meeting in the UK

Five ways to succeed

Be clear why the meeting is necessary.

Only relevant people should attend the meeting.

Book meeting rooms and facilities early.

Keep to an agreed date and time.

Send regular reminders to delegates.

Five ways to fail

Be unclear about the purpose of the meeting.

■ Don't check and chase up attendance.

■ Don't check layout and organisation of the meeting room.

Don't send out invitations.

Ignore the paperwork (agenda, minutes).

Why...?

Welcome to the world of meetings. This is the activity which will take up the majority of your time at work. Up to 60 per cent, in fact. An estimated four million hours are spent in meetings *every day* in the UK alone.

So now you've realised this is likely to be your major work activity you need to know how to organise your time. The best way to do this is to use the time-honoured framework of five *W*'s and an *H: Why, What, Who, When, Where* and *How.* Let's start with *Why.*

Why so many meetings? Good question. Meetings are like tribal gatherings. Work groups share a practical and emotional need to get together and discuss things and to exchange information.

You may not have much choice about which meetings you attend, but even meetings you think are irrelevant may be useful. You get the opportunity to observe how meetings work. Remember, don't just focus on the topic, focus on the mechanics of the meeting (how it's constructed and run) as well.

Meetings are the lifeblood of any organisation. They are the way information is shared in the group. They are the prime way of giving the work group a sense of belonging. This is why it's worth:

■ limiting the number of meetings

■ having more focused meetings

■ having shorter meetings.

Let's unpack each item on that list.

Limit the number of meetings

Attend four two-hour meetings back to back and you'll know why you need to limit the number of meetings. Your whole working day has gone – and you haven't done any desk work yet. So you're already behind. In addition, by the end of the fourth meeting, what you discussed in the first meeting is a distant memory.

If you're lucky enough to be able to choose which meetings to attend, consider these criteria. Prioritise meetings which:

- directly concern you
- have information you need to know about
- cover responsibilities you have to report on
- contain people you need to meet or talk to
- deal with things which interest you or you can learn from.

For all the rest, take a view.

- Get a copy of the meeting invitation and the agenda. Does it meet one of your criteria above? If yes, try and go. If not, ask your line manager if you need to attend.

- Learn to discriminate. Decide which meetings will be important or helpful to you. For the others, explain your workload to your line manager and ask if you can be absent. Ask yourself constantly: 'What is my purpose for being here? Could I use this time better, doing something else?'

- Most meetings can be summarised over the coffee machine. If you miss a meeting, ask a colleague: 'Did I miss anything important?'

- If you did miss something important, get a copy of the minutes. If necessary and appropriate, follow up with your own views.

Types of meetings

Obviously, not all meetings are the same. The type of meeting will depend on its function. Let's look at some of them.

Tribal gatherings

These are fairly rare. They tend to be semi-public occasions and involve the paramount chief and various sub-chiefs. Each clan in the tribe is involved in praise songs and 'death to our enemy' chants, awards are handed out and there is some hospitality on hand. If you've attended an annual school prize-giving or sports day you'll know what we're talking about. In a company it's usually called the AGM (Annual General Meeting), new product launch, or something like that. Why go? You go for the jamboree and the hospitality. It's also a good chance to network, and if you're to be honoured with a prize like 'employee of the year', it's probably worth a look-in.

Weekly or monthly updates

These are usually project team and departmental meetings. Their function is to update on activities, check progress against deadlines, allocate responsibilities, troubleshoot problems and make sure everyone knows what they are supposed to be doing. Why go? You need to attend these. They're important. If you can't attend, make sure people know beforehand. 'No shows' are not well viewed. It's a sign of disinterest or failure of responsibility. Neither are recommended qualities for promotion. So remember: if you can't go, let the chair know. Beforehand.

Performance reviews

Performance reviews are another type of meeting. You often have to prepare paperwork, and sometimes the outcome of this meeting affects your salary, bonuses and training opportunities.

Brainstorms

These are single topic discussions with an open agenda where all ideas are welcome. The rule (not always observed) is that any idea, no matter how far-fetched, is worth voicing. The aim is to get ideas for future action, often in new areas of company development. Why go? They're lively and fun and they help you get a feeling for other members of the group: how they think; what their priorities are. If you have something useful to contribute it's also a great way to make an impression. One word of advice: never speak first. You're better off keeping your powder dry until you know which way the wind is blowing. Then when you do speak, in favour or in opposition to what others are saying, you'll make a stronger impact.

General meetings

If these don't sound relevant to you, avoid them whenever you can. They can range from how to economise on coffee machines to saving paper or other office matters. Enough said.

Shorter meetings

Let's practise what we preach and have a brief summary of shorter meetings. Here are three ideas:

- **Meeting at 10.10** Most people expect ten o'clock. They wander in a few minutes late, get coffee or tea, find their seat, complain that there are no biscuits, and catch up on gossip. So the first ten minutes or so is actually wasted time. That's why some meeting organisers start their meetings at an odd time. They start at ten minutes past ten, ignore latecomers and don't recap for them. They get on with the agenda and finish when they say they will. If there is anything not discussed, they do it in a private meeting later or put it back to the next meeting.

- **Stand-up meetings** That's right. No one sits down. After half an hour or less, people are sagging – a great way to shorten a meeting, though not very comfortable.

- **Timed agenda** Some meeting organisers put a duration against each point on the agenda, e.g. *holiday time announcement (5 mins)*. This used to be very popular but has fallen out of favour now. Still useful, though, if only as an indicator.

If you think short meetings are impossible, look at the agenda of the President of the United States: *Affairs of State may be concluded in ten minutes.* No time for chat there.

Other meetings

Not all meetings take place in an office. If you work in a factory or department store, team meetings and staff announcements will often be held on the factory or sales floor. How are they different? Most meetings will be shorter. Most people will be standing up. They will usually be run by the department head, team leader or, maybe, trade union official.

The atmosphere is likely to be much more informal. People will just stand around the speaker. Once the announcement is made, people can ask questions. Then, when it's over, everyone simply goes back to work.

In many factories and department stores, team 'huddles' are popular. These are informal meetings at the beginning or end of the day to remind the team of important points and boost morale.

There's a last type of meeting that takes place in public. This is when senior members of staff address the troops on more general policy issues. These might take place in the cafeteria or in another public space. Do go. It might be your only chance to see the boss in person!

What ...?

Meetings start with an invitation. The invitation is usually an email, sent round to people to say the meeting will take place. The invitation will normally state:

- Date
- Time (start and finish)
- Location (room/building, check the size/capacity of the room)
- Participants in the meeting
- Topic (what the key aim of the meeting is, e.g. management meeting, conference planning, work allocation on the shop floor, customer service procedure, etc.)
- Contact person (the person arranging the meeting)

If the agenda is finalised, it's a very good idea to attach it to the invitation.

See Step 2 for more on invitations.

Who ...?

One of the key questions in any meeting is who should attend. There is a golden rule: *as few as possible*. And only those relevant to the outcome. Allowing everybody in is rarely effective in a meeting. You end up with dozens of ideas, hundreds of disagreements, no decisions and no clear way forward.

What are the outcomes of this approach?

- time wasted
- disaffected people
- a demotivated department

It's far better to decide what you want to achieve and who you think will help you achieve it, as well as those who might oppose it, though you need to listen to them. They often think of things you forget or warn you of possible dangers. Get these people in the meeting and focus on them.

How many people should attend? Research suggests that the optimum number of people in any meeting is five or seven: an odd number of participants allows a majority view to be reached. Many directors hold pre-meetings, almost chats, with trusted colleagues (and opponents) to review options and strategies before taking the issue to the larger meeting.

When...?

As you'd expect, if we spend 60 per cent of our time in meetings, there's a lot of research into the right time for the meeting. Believe it or not, it varies. Most people will argue 10 or 11 a.m., when people are fresh. Almost everybody agrees that 2 p.m. after lunch is not the ideal time, but many meetings are held at 4 or 5 p.m. and they work quite well as 'end of day' team round-ups.

But you have to check availability times. As an example, the contract hours of the British employees in a French company in London were 8 a.m. to 5.45 p.m. The French would arrive at about 9.30, have a decent lunch from 12.45 to 2 p.m. and then leave the office around 7 or 7.30 p.m. As a result, they held their team meetings at 6 p.m.

This was like a French red rag to a British bull. This wasn't just inconsiderate. It was a plot to make the British stay late at the office or cut them out of the decision-making loop. Office politics at its worst!

In fact, it was just a mistake. The French simply didn't think. Once they realised the problem, they brought the team meeting forward to 4.30. Harmony reigned once again.

Punctuality is important in UK business. It's important to be on time for meetings. If you think you might be late, always phone. Say you will be a bit later than you need. It's much better to call and say, 'I'll be 20 minutes late', and arrive earlier.

There are lots of examples like the French one, especially in companies with employees from different countries. 'Who's holding a meeting on my national day?' 'Who wants me to work on Sunday?' (Not uncommon in Middle Eastern companies, where the holy day is Friday.) 'Who wants me to go to a meeting at six o'clock in Ramadan?' Sensitivity to issues like these helps employees feel considered and makes them more willing to come to meetings.

Normally, meetings conform to the holiday conventions of the UK. However, in our increasingly multinational working environment, it's important to acknowledge others' festivals and celebrations. The Chinese New Year is a good example of this.

Finding out about alternative dates can be a challenge. A good way to organise a meeting is to use a time chart.

Name	Date 6th June Time 11.00 a.m.	Date 7th June Time 11.00 a.m.	Date 17th June Time 11.00 a.m.
John	*	*	*
Hilary			
Pia			
Barry			

The time chart is a table with names of invitees, dates and time. The organiser circulates it to colleagues. Notice there is an asterisk against the three dates. This indicates that the organiser, John, is free. The others do the same and when there is a day where all the slots are filled, then that is the day of the meeting. Simple but effective. Most computers have programs designed to help you arrange meetings and view people's availability.

What happens if the spaces aren't filled by everyone? Try again. It may take two or three attempts.

Where ....?

Where to hold a meeting poses two problems. One is whether to hold it inside or outside the office. The other is room and layout.

Office or elsewhere?

Most people think the right place to hold a meeting is around a table in an office. But meetings can take place anywhere. Some take place in the break-out areas in offices (the more informal areas with sofas and bean bags). See Step 5 for more information on informal meetings. Others take place in hotel lobbies or in restaurants over lunch or dinner. There are also away-days that are purposely arranged so they are off-site, i.e. away from the office, often in a business centre, so that people can get away from their day job and think about bigger picture issues.

If the groundwork for a meeting is done in a more relaxing environment, the formal bit, the confirmation, if you like, can be done in the office.

The office isn't always the best place to start a series of meetings. It is usually the best place to finish them.

One of the key advantages of meetings outside the office is that participants are not so likely to get sucked into everyday office business. For example, if training sessions are held in the office training room there is a constant temptation to nip back to the office to check messages and make phone calls during the breaks. Obviously, participants can still access messages on their mobiles or laptops but off-site training means the interruptions will be fewer and briefer.

Meeting room organisation and layout

Dedicated meeting rooms should be OK for your meeting. But do check. They may be festooned with wires for conference calls or have computers on every desk.

Check the room you've booked is the right size and has enough chairs. And also check it doesn't have too many chairs. Twenty chairs round a table when you have a meeting of five may make the place feel a bit empty. A bit like a restaurant with too many waiters and no guests. Check what's in the room and around the walls. Is there anything you'd prefer your meeting attendees not to see? Also check the facilities. Is the space clean? Are the rubbish bins empty? Is the whiteboard clean? Is there a flipchart? Do you need data projection facilities?

When you've got your room, check the layout. Different kinds of layouts work for different kinds of activity. See page 20 for the different layouts.

Boardroom

When you see the US government around the table in the White House in Washington DC or the Cabinet room at Number 10 Downing Street, the British Prime Minister's residence and office in London, you're looking at a boardroom layout. It's good for limited discussion and creating a collective atmosphere.

The leader or convenor of a meeting is often called *the chair* (a unisex term).

Here's a useful tip. If you want to get noticed in a meeting, make sure you are within the eyeline of the meeting leader. Just opposite or slightly to the right or left facing them is probably best.

Circle

Circles are for togetherness and for exchange. People in a circle, without tables, are favoured by 'self-development' groups. It's supposed to encourage the exchange of personal information in a more relaxed environment. Going back to our meetings-as-tribal-gatherings analogy, American Indian pow-wows (discussions) were traditionally held in a circle. Traditional African village discussions are held in a circle under a tree in the village 'square', often with the leader in the middle holding a shell or other symbol giving him/her the right to speak. The Roman Senate sat in a circle and the United Nations and the EU debating chambers each form a semi-circle. Circles and semi-circles stress togetherness. Rows facing each other stress opposition – hence the layout of the British House of Commons.

Horseshoe

The horseshoe also encourages discussion, but also allows more space and freedom. Horseshoes work well for brainstorming and open discussion and have the advantage that all participants can see each other and address each other, with no one in a superior position.

Cabaret

Cabaret layouts work well for meetings where there are 12 or more participants, and they are seated around tables for three or four, a bit like tables in a nightclub – hence the name cabaret. A cabaret layout allows for lots of group work and reporting back.

Theatre

For large groups, sitting in rows might be the best way to proceed. It's difficult to have group discussion in a theatre layout though. It's best for listening to a presentation and asking and answering questions afterwards (Q&A).

Facing rows

Avoid this one if you can. It promotes opposition, as mentioned earlier. The British parliamentary system is based on government versus opposition. So it's noisy and, in a fairly friendly British way, antagonistic.

The same occurs in business, but it's not always friendly. Sometimes, this layout is dictated by the shape of the room and the number of attendees. The danger is that if people are opposite each other, they will naturally sit with those they agree with and opposite those they don't.

As an example: a firm had contractual difficulties with one of its affiliates. A meeting was arranged to try to resolve the problem. Unfortunately, the meeting room had a table with two rows of chairs facing each other. The contractor and her team sat on one side and the affiliate and his team on the other. The atmosphere was stiff and cold. Points of agreement were difficult to find.

Then the contractor had a brainwave. She suggested they take a break, and during the break she changed the meeting room. The new room had a round table! Immediately, there was a more positive atmosphere, and after more discussion both sides reached an agreement.

What had changed? The meeting leader was convinced of one thing. Sitting round a table in a circle diminished the atmosphere of confrontation and increased the willingness to cooperate.

Meeting room layouts

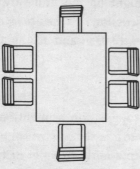

Boardroom

Circle

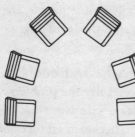

Horseshoe

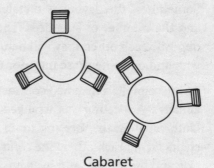

Cabaret

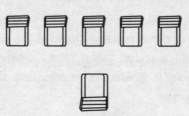

Theatre

As a final thought, have you ever watched *The Apprentice*? Think what you've learned about meeting organisation and room layout – how does it apply to what you've seen on the show? At first, it's lovey dovey. Lord Sugar arrives in his Bentley. He stands in front of the teams, mixes them up and gives them the task. Fifty minutes later, it's another story. He sits at a desk in front of a frosted glass door, flanked by his cohorts. Opposite him in two rows sit or stand the two teams. There aren't enough seats for everyone.

It's a mixture of theatre style, in this case more like a classroom, and facing rows. The two teams aren't actually facing each other, but it feels very oppositional – almost like a courtroom. The layout seems designed for maximum superiority (Lord Sugar) and maximum humiliation (the contestants).

This is nothing to do with Lord Sugar, but everything to do with the production values which, *Big Brother* style, try to create tension and conflict in order to build audiences. The age of the gladiator is not dead! But it's exactly the wrong way to set up and run a meeting.

Imagine if the approach was cooperative and aimed at showing everyone at their best. People would sit next to, not opposite each other. They would discuss in a circle, a horseshoe or cabaret style, not in facing rows. Lord Sugar and his cohorts would sit among the contestants, not apart from them.

Layout determines whether the atmosphere will be collaborative or confrontational.

How ...?

So let's imagine you are asked to organise a meeting. What? No! That'll never happen to you! Well, actually it might. An intern was asked to organise the weekly management meeting. Why? It was a good way to test her organising skills and her willingness to take responsibility and use her initiative. She came through with flying colours and, as a result of this and her other work, got an offer of a permanent job.

What did she do? She used the framework. Five *W*'s and an *H*:

- **WHY?** First she asked why the meeting was necessary. What was it intended to achieve?

- **WHAT?** Then she checked the topic. That would go on the invitation.

- **WHO?** Then she asked who needed to be invited, names and job titles. She double-checked these. (Her life would have been a misery if she had got them wrong!)

- **WHEN?** Her line manager suggested a time, but she needed to check alternatives. She used a time chart to check everyone's availability and found a date and time that suited everyone.

- **WHERE?** She had to decide whether to hold the meeting in the office or outside the office. In the event, her line manager preferred the office. So she booked a room, checked it, moved the tables and chairs around, ensured there was a data projector and booked tea, coffee, biscuits and a sandwich lunch from the canteen.

■ **HOW?** What needs to happen?

Having decided on the *Why, What, Who, When* and *Where,* the intern finally had to deal w'th the *How.* What did she need to do?

1 Book a room.

2 Send out the invitations.

3 Chase up anyone who hadn't replied.

4 Circulate the agenda and any papers to be 'tabled' (discussed).

5 Chase up anybody who hadn't replied (there'll always be a few).

6 Check the room was OK for the meeting. Raid the stationery cupboard (for any pens/paper the participants will need).

7 Telephone attendees to remind them.

8 Make a note of those who would be absent or would have to leave early.

9 Prepare the agenda (see Step 2).

How does this apply to you?

As the intern realised, organising a meeting is both a challenge and an opportunity. If you get the opportunity, how do you meet the challenge? First, find out what has been done before. Ask more experienced colleagues or your line manager.

Secondly, think of your own experience. If you've participated in meetings before, is there anything you can use? Thirdly, don't worry about inexperience. This is an opportunity to learn. It's also an opportunity to show you can take responsibility and show initiative.

Lastly, after the meeting, take time to reflect. What have you learned from the experience? What will you do, say, and above all, think in the future? Learning to reflect on your experience and learn lessons for the future is one of the most important things you can do as an employee.

Key take-aways

Think about the things you will take away from Step 1 and how you will implement them.

Topic	Take-away	Implementation
How to assess whether meetings are relevant	• *Not all meetings are relevant. Some are just routine.*	• *Ask my line manager to prioritise.*
How to make the most of meetings you have to attend		
How to recognise types of meeting		
How to keep meetings shorter		
How to write a good meeting invitation		
How to decide who to invite		
How to check availability		
How to make sure the room is suitable		
How to organise a meeting practically		
How to manage what you have learned		

Step 2

PREPARE USEFUL DOCUMENTS

*'Whoever controls the minutes,
controls the meeting!' — UK finance manager*

Five ways to succeed

Always have an agenda.

Communicate the aim and objectives.

Organise the discussion documents for the meeting.

Know how to present your own ideas.

Take and present minutes to suit the meeting.

Five ways to fail

Assume the meeting can run by itself.

Waste time by not organising/attaching discussion papers.

Fail to ask someone to take the minutes.

Write down what everyone says and then try to reproduce it.

Forget to check minutes before circulation.

The need for documentation

Good meetings depend on planning and successful planning depends partly on good documentation.

Four key documents will contribute to a successful meeting. They are:

- The invitation
- The agenda
- Supporting papers and discussion documents
- The minutes

The invitation makes sure you get the right people in the right place on the right day at the right time.

The agenda is your roadmap to success. It is the path to meeting the goals and objectives of your meeting. It ensures you clarify your meeting objectives and it identifies the process you need to go through to achieve them with the relevant stakeholders.

The supporting papers and discussion documents provide the necessary background to any discussion, but need to be presented in an unambiguous and accessible way.

The minutes are not just a record of the meeting. They are an action plan going forward.

Clear, relevant and action-oriented action points provide the platform for the next steps.

There should be a clear progression from the agenda to the minutes. The order of the minutes should reflect the order of the agenda and should clearly relate to the subject headings and issues raised in each item. If it doesn't, you risk confusion.

The invitation

When you prepare an invitation, you tell attendees about the meeting: where they need to go, what date and what time.

Sounding pro: Meeting invitations

Here's an example of an invitation:

To:
From:
Re: Team meeting

Dear Colleagues,

We are holding two meetings in May to discuss reorganisation of the department. It is extremely important that everyone in the team attends. We are proposing two dates: May 17th or May 24th at 1 p.m. in the canteen. Please let me know by May 6th which date or dates you are available for.

I look forward to hearing from you. Thank you.

Sara Leboeuf
HR Manager

Why is this invitation successful?

■ It's clear – it states the type of meeting.

■ It explains – it doesn't take for granted that the participants know.

■ It specifies attendance – it says who should come.

■ It offers alternative time slots.

■ It offers a choice of dates.

■ It's polite and it makes clear requests with a clear deadline.

■ It shows authority – the sender states her job title at the end.

The invitation also creates a record. Do people need a record? If you've got back-to-back meetings or very few meetings, yes, you do. Knowing where you have to be and when is all important.

■ Date

Write it how you like. Some people prefer *May 6th 2013*. Some like *6th May 2013*. Many people, even in the UK, use the US form *6 May 2013* or *May 6 2013*.

You may see this: *6/7/13* (the 6th of July 2013), but be careful, as in America and other parts of the world, the month comes first, like this: *7/6/13* (the 6th of July 2013) not, as it looks to the British (the 7th of June 2013).

If in doubt, copy the format from a previous meeting.

■ Time

Just to be clear, many companies now use the 24-hour clock and write the time as part of a 24-hour period. So 09:05 is five minutes past nine a.m. and 12:05 is five minutes past 12 o'clock midday. Alternatively, you can use a.m./p.m.

It's important to note that people from different cultures have different attitudes to time. Some are much more tolerant of delays and lateness than others. The UK, by and large, is an 'on time' culture. It's much better to arrive five minutes early for a meeting than five minutes late. Also, if you're going to be late you should ring and advise as early as possible.

■ Location

This is straightforward: building, address (if needed) and room number, e.g.

Room 101
Edinburgh Building
3 East Side
Nottingham

Be careful you get numbers and addresses right. If the meeting is in your office building, check the room booked corresponds to the room number on the invitation and agenda.

If the meeting is off-site (i.e. away from the office), check the directions (they are sometimes called joining instructions) are easy to follow. Do get it right. It's all too easy to send people to the wrong room or even to the wrong building on the wrong side of town!

Check and double-check the details are right. If you're in the same building, nip along and check. Fifteen minutes spent now might save hours of wasted time and frustration later – for you and the participants. After all, you don't want to end up on the roof!

Requesting items for inclusion

Sometimes the invitation may include a request for items to be discussed by the participants. Imagine this situation. You had an action point from the last meeting that you haven't been able to complete. So you want to have further discussion in the next meeting. The best way to do this may be to put it on the agenda for the meeting.

It's worth asking all participants if they want to include this or perhaps another item. You can either do this when you send out the invitation or else in a separate email, once the meeting date has been agreed.

Date:
All addressees:
Subject: Agenda items for meeting on 28th March

Dear all,
Please let me have any agenda items for the meeting on 28th March by 5 p.m. on 25th March.

Thank you very much.
Tom Hadfield

Types of meeting

Before we go on to the next piece of documentation, the agenda, let's make a distinction between two types of meeting. The first is the regular meeting. This is a meeting of a project team or department which takes place at regular intervals, weekly or monthly. The aim of the meeting is primarily to update on progress and troubleshoot problems. This is the kind of meeting where the meeting leader may request items for inclusion, as above.

The second is a 'one-off' meeting to discuss a particular topic or issue. In this case, there has been no 'last meeting' and therefore it's unlikely, though not impossible, that the meeting leader will request items for inclusion.

The agenda

Agendas are the single organising principle of a business meeting. They define what needs to be discussed and in what order. They are therefore the starting point for any successful meeting, and the lack of one is the main starting point for an unsuccessful meeting. But they also have another function. They help you organise your thoughts. When you write an agenda, automatically you think about what you want to agree on. These are the aims and objectives of the meeting.

If you look around, you'll see business people in informal meetings in coffee shops, cafés and restaurants. Even for informal meetings they'll ask the question, 'What do we need to discuss?' And they will scribble the points to discuss on a napkin or piece of paper. It may not look like it, but that's an agenda.

The way to focus a meeting is through the agenda. Agendas help you think more constructively and more logically about what you want to achieve. It's not just about organising your thoughts. It's also about deciding what order you want to present them in – the progression. Going into a meeting without a clear agenda is like going into a meeting without a focus.

Agendas – what to include

Agendas are often included with the invitation. They normally include the following information:

Details of meeting, date, time, location

See pages 28 and 29.

Participants

This is a list of who is expected at the meeting, the participants. At the very least, write their names, but some agendas include job titles too.

Once again, your policy should be to look at a previous agenda and check how people are described. Use that as your guide. Expect at least the full first name and family name, e.g. *Barry Tomalin*.

In more formal meetings, titles may be attached, e.g. *Mr Barry Tomalin, M.A.* However, check gender. Is Hilary Baker a man or a woman? Check company policy. Mentioning gender titles may be politically incorrect.

In some cases, job titles may also be added, e.g. *Alicia Jones, R&D Coordinator EMEA*.

So here is your next problem, acronyms. What does an R&D Coordinator do? And what is EMEA? R&D is Research and Development, in other words, a researcher. EMEA defines the region of responsibility. It stands for Europe, Middle East and Africa. Part of your background research is to note the names (people you may never meet but you are expected to know who they are), their job titles and the acronyms that describe their areas of responsibility. Information may be found on the company intranet. Never be afraid to ask about this, especially during your first few months in the company. But don't be surprised – they may not know either!

Apologies for absence

Some people don't turn up for meetings and they don't tell anyone beforehand. In Britain, in particular, this is not well viewed, and in France they call it *absence sauvage*: 'savage absence'. If you can't make a meeting, you should always email or phone in good time. If it's a short notice cancellation or delay, make sure you phone.

If by any chance you miss a meeting and don't inform the meeting leader, then you should apologise by phone or email as soon as possible afterwards.

On the agenda, absence is noted like this:

Apologies   Or:
Barry Tomalin   *Apologies received from Barry Tomalin*

Or:
Apologies received
Barry Tomalin

If you've sent your apologies in advance, then you should be on the list to receive the minutes of the meeting. If for any reason you don't receive them, then you should ask for them.

33

Minutes of last meeting

For a regular meeting, when you send out the invitation to the next meeting, you should usually attach the minutes of the previous meeting. That way everyone can check what has and hasn't been done since the last meeting.

Agenda items

Each item on the agenda has a title, for example:

1. *Project update (Claire) – (7 minutes), Paper 2.1*

Check company practice in the presentation of items.

- Is an 'item owner' listed? In this case, Claire introduces the update, followed by discussion.
- Is there a suggested time? This proposes a theoretical duration for the presentation and discussion. It helps the meeting leader keep track of time, so he/she can shorten the discussion or cut another item lower down the list. Also, it helps the item owner, Claire, know how long she is expected to take.
- Are there supporting papers? If so, it may be useful to list these so that participants know which paper refers to which item.

The number of items on the agenda depends on the time available and the number of issues to be discussed. But an agenda of seven items in a 60-minute meeting would be ample.

Supporting papers may be of different types. They might include financial statements, product specifications and descriptions, and position papers on issues of policy or strategy. They can be added to the agenda and circulated with it as hard or soft copy. Be sure to have hard copies on hand for participants who haven't printed out the soft copy!

AOB (Any Other Business)

At the end of the meeting, the meeting leader goes round the table and asks: 'Is there any other business/AOB?' This is the opportunity for each participant to advise the group of matters outside the agenda. This might include further information that a participant thinks is relevant to the meeting. Or it could be information about planned absences or holidays, or about the department and its activities. This rather vague description could cover anything from catering facilities to issues related to the main content of the meeting.

An example: in a management meeting, an executive said under AOB, 'I've been reviewing departmental expense claims for the last quarter. Could the sales manager explain the expense claim of £500 on hospitality for visiting Chinese customers?' The questioner clearly meant, 'Was the sales manager extravagant?' Presumably, he wanted to embarrass the sales manager.

How do you deal with such an intervention? The meeting leader was quick off the mark: 'Thank you for the question,' she said. 'I suggest we discuss it outside the meeting. Let's move on.' Case closed.

Date of the next meeting

Usually, this is a formality. The meeting leader simply suggests a time and date for a follow-up meeting and everyone agrees. 'Date of next meeting? Next week, same day, same time, same place' is probably the simplest way to arrange it.

However, if not everyone is free, it may be a good moment to use a time chart (see Step 1) to find a time when the majority are free to attend.

Sounding pro: Agendas

We've discussed the invitation and the agenda. Here is what a standard agenda might look like:

Management Meeting
15 May 2013, 15:00–16:00
Room 101

Present
Sally Rogers (Chair)
Claire Bowles (Production)
Paul Ashcroft (Sales and Marketing)
Gerry Sloane (R&D)
Ben Davies (Finance)
Billie Emerson (Supply chain)
Martin McCulloch (IT)
Jamila Said (HR)

Apologies
John Holmes
Alicia da Silva

AGENDA
1 Department overview Q2 2013 (Sally)
2 Production update (Claire)
3 Sales and marketing update (Paul)
4 Financial report (Ben)
5 Supplier problems EMEA (Europe, Middle East, Africa) (Billie)
6 Upgrade of computer program for ordering and billing (Martin)
7 Recruitment of new sales assistants (Jamila)
8 AOB

Date of next meeting
22 May, 10:00–11:00

Discussion documents

The agenda is often accompanied by extra information documents which are circulated at the same time. These documents are intended for reading before the meeting and for discussion during the meeting. They may be called *discussion documents, position papers* or just *papers*. Each document refers to a different agenda item. Two things you need to consider are: organisation and preparation.

Organising discussion documents

If you are asked to prepare the paperwork for the meeting, you need to make sure of three things:

1 Have you got all the documentation that is required?

2 Is it numbered so participants can relate each document to the appropriate agenda item?

3 Have you put the documents in the order they appear on the agenda?

Give yourself time to get this right. Sorting it out is often a longer process than it looks.

Human nature means that you won't get all the papers for the meeting in good time. If you know there's a document to attach and you haven't got it yet, simply add a note to say 'document to follow', and that will do the job. Why does it matter? Remember: agendas are all about organising your thoughts before the meeting so you can get the best results out of the meeting itself. Attaching the right papers in the right order is part of this thought organising process.

Preparing discussion documents

You may be asked to prepare or review discussion documents to present at the meeting.

How do you go about it?

- **Think length first:** Most people think about what they want to say. It's more efficient to decide how much space you have and then plan your content.

- **Plan your headings:** Write a heading for each content point you want to make. This will help you organise your material to fit the space. Make sure the content headings include a conclusion.

- **Draft your content:** Write and fit the content to the page. Add your conclusion.

Imagine you have to prepare a paper to discuss as part of an agenda item. Imagine you've done your research, you've created graphs, charts and your commentary, but the result is quite long. What could you do to make it shorter? The answer is to add a cover page with two items: an executive summary and the key points, presented in bullet point format.

Sounding pro: Executive summary

The executive summary is a short summary of the conclusions and recommendations. You should start each line with a bullet point. The bullet points list the main points in your report and refer to the page number where the detailed information can be found. The whole thing is one page long. The other pages are the data.

Here is what an executive summary looks like:

New business opportunities

Agenda item 5: Attracting 18–25 year-olds to open bank accounts

Executive summary:

- *The bank wants to broaden its base of 18–25 year-old bank account holders. To do so successfully, it needs to identify key products that will appeal to the target market now and in the future.*

- *My research shows that 18–25 year-olds are graduates and apprentices starting out in their careers (report pp. 3–4). They need cash and manageable overdraft facilities plus credit card facilities. However, they also need something more (report pp. 5–6). Especially in the 22–25 age group, new entrants to the job market are interested in long-term security, savings, mortgage and, in some cases, retirement benefits (pp. 7–8).*

- *My recommendation is that the bank does a publicity campaign to offer a range of both short- and long-term benefits as an incentive to banking with us.*

Short term	*Long term*
* *credit card*	* *savings*
* *free online banking*	* *insurance*
* *overdraft facility*	* *pension*
* *local events invitations*	* *mortgage*

Minutes

The minutes is a record of the meeting. It creates a 'paper trail', a record you can follow of who agreed to do what, when and how, and what the result was. It is the crucial meetings document. That said, there are many ways of writing minutes. Here are three of the most common minutes formats.

1 Who, what, when: This is the simplest format. For each agenda point, the minute-taker simply lists the following information:

- **What?** What action points were agreed.
- **Who?** Who is responsible for implementing the action points.
- **When?** When the action points should be done by.

Often the answer to 'when' is simply 'Report at next meeting.'

2 Summary of main points: This is a slightly more detailed minutes format. It lists the agenda points and the main points made in the discussion, usually with a reference to the person who made the point. This enables participants to check what they said and refresh their memory of the meeting.

It's also helpful for people who weren't at the meeting and want to know about the discussion. Some companies circulate the minutes to people who weren't at the meeting. Those people may have the right to add to or amend the minutes, even though they weren't there.

3 Blow-by-blow: This format is for more general discussion when it's considered important to record different opinions about an issue of policy or strategy. This may be useful for future reference as it allows for detailed information of who said what.

Who should take the minutes?

In many meetings, the meeting leader takes the minutes. This is not a good idea. It is difficult to focus on and control the discussion and take the minutes. A member of the group should take them.

How to take the minutes

You need a keen ear. You have to listen carefully and note the points that need to be minuted. You have to capture the essence of the meeting. For example, sometimes you have to reflect the feeling of the meeting regarding key issues raised. It demands concentration, and sometimes courage. You may have to interrupt the meeting and pause the discussion to ask for clarification. You may need to ask the meeting leader, 'What shall I minute?' at the end of the discussion.

Above all, you support the meeting leader. Your intervention, 'What shall I minute?' gives the meeting leader an excuse to halt a discussion, and move on. The minutes are crucial, so if someone asks you to take them, don't see it as a chore.

When taking the minutes of the meeting, focus on what, who and when for each agenda item. Make sure they are precise, with a clear layout.

Apply these rules:

- **Be concise:** One thought per sentence.
- **Be brief:** Keep sentences to 15–25 words. Could one long sentence be two short ones?
- **Pay attention to thought space:** Begin each thought in a different paragraph. It creates mental space for the reader.
- **Pay attention to line space:** A line between each paragraph. Use 1.5 line spacing, if you can.

You can sum up these four rules in one acronym – KISS: 'Keep it short and simple.'

Sounding pro: Minutes

Here's a simple layout for minutes:

MINUTES

MEETING: *Attracting new accounts (young adults)*

DATE: *28 May*

VENUE: *Cornwall Building, Room 304*

PARTICIPANTS: *Joan Pratt, Manager Business Banking; Tim Saumarez, Regional Publicity Manager; Joyce Awolowo, Human Resources Manager*

APOLOGIES: *George Arthur, Regional Banking*

ACTION POINTS:

1 *New business opportunities – young adults*
   Action point: Prepare offer for new accounts (Responsible: Joan)
   When: Present at next Board meeting on June 6th

2 *Publicity for new accounts*
   Action point: Commission leaflet and online publicity from advertising agency (Responsible: Tim)
   When: Follow-up on approval of offering

3 *Recruitment to manage new accounts*
   Action point: Business case for new appointment – new accounts manager (Responsible: Joyce)
   When: Report at next meeting

4 *AOB: Alice on maternity leave from end of month. Temporary replacement being advertised.*

DATE OF NEXT MEETING: *11 June*

Finalising the minutes

If you're the minute-taker or the meeting leader, get together as soon as possible to agree the minutes while the discussion is still fresh. Some minute-takers actually write the minutes on their laptop during the meeting. This allows instant feedback between the meeting leader and minute-taker. We'll deal with what you do with the minutes after they've been circulated in Step 7.

Who circulates the minutes?

Did you note the quote at the beginning of Step 2: 'Whoever controls the minutes, controls the meeting'? This is especially important in 'blow-by-blow' meetings when people's opinions are reported in more detail. As minute-taker, you can decide what's important and what isn't so important, within limits.

Since the minutes are the record of the meeting, they are all anyone will remember, except the speaker, of course. So what can you do to make sure they are accurate? Do these two checks:

■ If you're a participant, check the minutes report the message you wanted to convey accurately. If they don't, telephone the person responsible for taking the minutes and correct them. Remember, the words may be correct but the message may be distorted.

■ If you're the minute-taker, give the minutes to the meeting leader. You circulate them when he/she agrees them, but not before.

If the agenda is the starting point of the meeting, the minutes are the end point. They are what everybody refers to if there is any disagreement. So it's worth making sure they're an accurate record of what was agreed. The challenge is to be thorough and accurate while also being quick to prepare them for prompt circulation.

Key take-aways

Think about the things you will take away from Step 2 and how you will implement them.

Topic	Take-away	Implementation
How to produce a clear invitation	• *Include all relevant information, e.g. topic, date, place, time and participants.*	• *Check all information before circulating.*
How to make sure the purpose of the meeting is clear		
How to create an organised agenda		
How to ensure documents are consistent with the agenda		
How to ensure general circulation of meetings documentation		
How to organise the minutes		
How to take the minutes		
How to prioritise what to minute		

Step 3

PARTICIPATE WITH IMPACT

'Football is a team game. So is life.'
— Joe Namath, American football player

Five ways to succeed

Be polite and cheerful at all times.

Find ways to involve yourself in the meeting.

Think before you speak.

■ Keep your remarks concise – short, sharp and sweet.

In disagreement, separate the person from the problem.

Five ways to fail

Be loud and argumentative.

Criticise the meeting leader openly.

■ Be too personal in your remarks.

Get upset and emotional.

Say nothing.

Active participation

In Step 6, we will look at the role of the meeting leader, but he/she isn't the only pebble on the beach. There is no meeting without the participants, and actively participating in a meeting involves a different set of skills from the meeting leader skills. Here, we'll look at how to be an effective participant and make a real impact. Let's review first of all what we've learned so far about participation.

■ **Demonstrate organisation and efficiency:** If you are asked to organise the meeting documentation, send out invitations and agendas and chase up participants, do it with as little fuss and as much efficiency as you can. Once again, your dedication to duty will be noticed.

■ **Never be afraid to ask questions:** If you're new to a task or job function, nobody expects you to completely understand it. It's much better to ask questions and get it right than do it and get it wrong.

■ **Learn from other's experience:** Observe what's happened before. Watch what others do. You may have a better way of doing it, but that comes later. Learn the conventions, and the reasons behind them, before you suggest changes.

■ **Keep cool:** Difficult to do, but it's important to remain calm and unflustered whatever the pressures. Remain positive and always look for solutions.

■ **Smile:** A smile works wonders. Smile even if you don't want to. People will respond to you much more positively.

Active listening

What is your key skill as a participant? Learn to listen. This is not just the most important participation skill, it's also the most important facilitation skill. But there's more to listening than meets the ear.

Minna was talking about her colleagues in staff meetings: 'People here just listen to the words you say,' she complained, 'but they never listen to the feelings.' What did she mean by that? Good listeners don't just hear what a person says, they focus on *how* they say it. Above all, they focus on how the person feels. As they listen, they try to pick up whether the person is enthusiastic or bored, happy or sad, passionate or indifferent, confident or nervous, positive or tentative. All these factors may influence the value and importance of their contribution and will determine the response. This demands acute concentration on the *person*, not just on the words.

This process is called active listening – listening to the feelings as well as the words. But when you practise active listening, what do you listen for? Four things: the tone of voice; the feelings; the body language (eye contact, hands, facial expression, body posture); and last of all, the words.

Experts identify four listening styles:
- non-listeners: only interested in the sound of their own voice
- marginal listeners: only listen to you as a take-off pad to launch into their own views
- pretend listeners: listen to you but judge what you're saying; they hear the words not the feelings, as Minna says above
- active listeners: this is what you should aim to be.

Tone of voice

When you listen to the tone of voice, you focus on the intonation pattern; whether the voice is tight (nervous) or loose (confident). In other words, you're listening to the tone of the speaker. A high-pitched 'squeaky' tone could convey nervousness or it could convey excitement. A rich bass tone may convey confidence but it might also sound self-important.

Feelings

In a meeting, listen to the feelings the speaker displays, particularly confidence or nervousness. Or it could be anger or passion – it's important to distinguish between the two, as they can sound very similar. Usually your instinct will tell you. If you're not sure, it's best simply to note that the other person has strong feelings and not to react angrily.

Body language

When you're in a meeting, watch the speaker's body language. This includes eye contact, facial expressions, hand gestures and body posture. If the speaker looks down and avoids eye contact, it might suggest lack of confidence or that they don't really believe what they're saying. If they look at the ceiling it might suggest they're trying to find their words.

Eye contact: Make eye contact with each participant in the meeting. But be careful: to some people it might suggest anger and aggression, especially if it looks like you're 'staring somebody out'. Also, remember that in some countries sustained eye contact is considered rude, especially to meeting participants who are higher ranking than you. Looking the senior person 'in the eye' may be seen as disrespectful and challenging.

Hands: Hands can also be a giveaway: people may fidget with their hands or click a ballpoint pen as they speak. This may indicate nervousness or impatience. Far better to sit with your hands on the table, using them only to make small gestures to emphasise a point. 'Hand-washing' is also a common gesture in meetings: participants rubbing their hands together may not mean what they say. Be careful of people sitting back with their arms folded. This may tell you that the person is closed to your ideas.

Facial expression: Another thing to watch out for is facial expression. We all know about the 'rictus smile', the smile through gritted teeth when you deliver bad news or say something unpleasant but want to hide it. But there may be other expressions, such as raised eyebrows, which show surprise or disbelief, or a firm unsmiling expression. We often think this shows disapproval, but it may equally show concentration.

Body posture: How people sit can reveal their attitude. Sitting forward may be a sign of engagement in the meeting, but sitting back may indicate lack of interest. Another sign of disengagement may be when people leaf through meeting documents, or, worse still, check their emails on their phones!

The words

After all this, we finally come to the words. As you listen, don't just listen to what the person is saying, listen to what they're *not* saying. They may be hiding bad news, or avoiding the disadvantages of their case.

From all this, you can see that active listening is all about observation – watching as well as listening.

The Mehrabian experiment

The psychologist, Dr Albert Mehrabian, conducted tests on US college students to see what listeners noted about the people they met. Mehrabian discovered that in any message the key communication is non-verbal. Of the three components of any spoken communication – words, tone of voice and body language – the most important was body language. Indeed, Mehrabian concluded that only 7 per cent of meaning is conveyed by words alone: 38 per cent is conveyed by tone of voice, but 55 per cent of meaning is conveyed by body language. Let's highlight that. In any communication:

- 7 per cent of meaning comes from what you say, the words

- 38 per cent of meaning comes from your tone of voice

- 55 per cent of meaning comes from your body language, how you feel when you speak.

This is why active listening, listening and watching for the feelings behind the words, is so important.

Rules of the road

You are participating in a meeting. You have earned your place at the table. Perhaps you're responsible for taking the minutes. How do you behave? Let's recap:

■ Respond to the invitation.

■ Dress right. Find out or ask about the dress code for the meeting. Don't stand out. If you're overdressed (suit and tie or posh frock when everyone else is in smart casual) or underdressed (jeans and T-shirt) you'll stand out in the wrong way. Sometimes people overdress because they have a more formal engagement after the meeting. If you're in this position, be prepared to explain.

■ Don't be late. Arrive for the meeting five minutes early. If you think you're going to be late, *always* phone or text and tell someone.

■ Do your homework. Carefully read any documentation circulated before the meeting. Make sure you understand the issues.

■ If you don't understand something before the meeting, ask. Especially, when you're new in a company, it's a good opportunity to make yourself known and show you're eager to learn.

■ Look attentive. It's good to show you're taking an interest. Focus on the meeting leader or whoever is speaking.

■ Take notes. It will help you remember key points you may want to follow up after the meeting.

■ Say hello. When you arrive, don't just stand or sit there, say hello to the people you know and to at least one person you don't know. Say something like: 'I just wanted to introduce myself. I'm Jamal, I'm in the design department and I work with Janie Hill.'

■ Mind your manners. Smile and be courteous. A positive attitude and courteous behaviour will add enormously to your prestige in meetings, especially in relation to older and more senior members of the group. Hold doors open. If you're getting tea, ask someone else if they would like one. If you interrupt, say, 'Sorry', and 'Please, carry on.' Remember that little courtesies are appreciated, but little rudenesses are not easily forgotten.

■ Age and seniority matter in some countries. In the UK, age and seniority don't automatically demand respect. In our increasingly egalitarian society, merit and results earn respect. However, this is not the case in much of the world, where age and seniority are respected as of right. If you have people of South Asian, East Asian, Middle Eastern or African backgrounds in your team, they may have different standards to you. Particularly if they are older and not born in the UK. Flippant remarks and rudeness about the boss may not be as funny or as irreverent to them as they are to you. They may be seen as just plain rude.

How to introduce yourself

This is the first challenge you may face when participating in a meeting. Often the meeting leader will call the meeting to order and say: 'Let's go round the table and introduce ourselves.' What do you say? Some people try to cram their life story into a minute and fail. It doesn't make a good impression. Others do just the opposite: 'Jones, Sales.' This is to the point, but makes no impression at all. Your aim is to give enough information so that people know who you are if they need to exchange information with you later or identify you if you make comments during the meeting. Americans call this the elevator pitch. Imagine you are in a lift with the managing director. You have about 20 seconds to introduce yourself. How do you do it?

When your turn comes to introduce yourself, make sure everyone can see you, smile and give the following information about yourself:

- name
- job title
- department
- who you work with/report to

Here's an example:

'Hi, my name's Sofia Benitez. I'm a marketing executive in the sales and marketing department, responsible for promotions. I'm working with Moira Lambert, Head of Publicity.'

That took 20 seconds. Job done. And in that 20 seconds people will know who you are and will remember you. They may also be impressed by your brevity and clarity.

How to intervene

Broadly speaking, there are three kinds of intervention. We'll look at each one in turn:

■ Checking information

■ Presenting an agenda item

■ Contributing to a discussion

Checking information

There are two occasions when you may need to do this. One is taking the minutes. The other is when you need repetition or clarification.

Taking the minutes is relatively straightforward, but if the meeting is heated or time is short, the meeting leader may forget to summarise and go straight on to the next point. If you are the minute-taker, remind the meeting leader to sum up the point. Confirm the *what* (action point), *who* (action point owner) and *when* (deadline for completion).

The second occasion is when you need repetition and clarification. The question is how much repetition? An example: a young French engineer at a project meeting got into trouble. An American spoke at length about some point. The French engineer asked for repetition. The American replied, 'Which bit?' The French engineer responded with, 'All of it!' Asking for clarification can sometimes be a bit tricky. The key is to make it clear you are not being critical, but asking out of interest, and to time your interruption so it's clear which bit you want clarification on: 'Could you clarify what you mean by that, please?' or 'Could you say a bit more about that, please?'

Presenting an agenda item

This is where you introduce an item on the agenda. The meeting leader announces the agenda item (let's imagine it's a new photocopier). He/she then asks you to introduce the item. The introduction may go like this: 'Right. Item 5. Jess, can you introduce this?' This is your cue. What do you say? Maybe you've already prepared paperwork and it was distributed with the papers for the meeting. In this case, the first thing you need to do is refer to the document concerned. Say something like: 'As you can see in the paperwork I circulated with the agenda, we've identified three possible photocopier suppliers.'

All reports have three components: the past, the present situation and future action. Don't talk for too long. The trick is to summarise the past briefly, explain the present situation and make proposals for future action with your recommendations. For example, you might say this:

■ **Past:** 'As you know, the photocopier wasn't meeting our requirements and we received a lot of complaints. We contacted the vendor but they didn't have the upgraded model we needed. So we were forced to look elsewhere.'

■ **Present:** 'We've surveyed staff needs and the key needs are clearly remote scanning and copying. We've identified three suppliers who meet our criteria regarding services and costs. Of these three, EasyTech seems to fit our needs best.'

■ **Future:** 'Next steps. Before we make a commitment, I would like to suggest we invite a representative to give a demonstration of their models at the next meeting.'

Contributing to a discussion

For some participants, this is the most terrifying part of a meeting. It's the moment when you raise your head above the parapet and expose yourself with all your weaknesses. It can even be difficult to find space to intervene if everyone is talking. So you need to do two things. The first is to create space to make your contribution. The second is to develop techniques of interrupting.

Creating space

Creating space to intervene can be a problem. In a busy meeting it may be difficult to get a word in edgeways if you want to present a proposal or make a comment. Here is a tip. Get hold of the agenda before the meeting, identify an item you want to contribute on and advise the meeting leader before the meeting.

How to interrupt

Even if the meeting leader forgets you wanted to contribute to an item, then a quick request from you in the meeting will remind him/her. However, there will also be times when you want to interrupt the meeting spontaneously in order to make a contribution. How do you do that? In this situation, the magic word is *just*. Why? Because it tells everybody you'll be quick. So you speak up and say: 'Could I just come in here?' or 'Could I just interrupt?' People will let you in because they think you'll be brief. When someone tries to interrupt you, once again, the magic word *just* comes to the rescue: 'Just let me finish' will defeat them.

Interrupting with respect

When you do interrupt, always make an effort to be polite and courteous. Treat the person you're interrupting or the person trying to interrupt you with respect. Failure to do so may give others a lasting bad impression of you.

Introductory phrases such as 'With respect' or 'With all due respect', used when you disagree, are nowadays often seen as a cliché meaning 'With no respect at all', but it is important to distinguish between the point you want to make and the person you want to make it to. Observe the rule: 'hard on the issue but soft on the person'.

How to catch the meeting leader's eye

Piping up as a lone voice in the wilderness may not be enough if no one can see you. It makes sense to sit opposite, or at least within the peripheral vision, of the meeting leader so he/she can see you. However, you may need to do more than just raise your voice. In this case, a gesture, such as a wave, may get the meeting leader's attention. It may feel like being back at school, but even raising your hand is a good way to get attention.

How to make your point

When you interrupt someone in a meeting, it's usually for one of four reasons:

- To ask a question
- To add a new point
- To share some information
- To disagree

Each reason has its own polite language and it's worth learning it. When you've learned it, you can adapt it with experience to suit your personal style.

Asking a question

The key to all interventions is diplomacy and tact. If you want to ask a question, ask permission. It may sound unnecessary, but simply adding: 'Could I ...' makes any question sound politer. It's also more likely to get a positive response. Say: 'Could I ask you to explain that in a bit more detail?'

Adding a new point

Quite often, when you interrupt someone in a meeting it's to add a point that everyone else has missed. You may begin by saying: 'Could I just add a point here?' (Note the magic word again.) It's helpful and diplomatic to make your position clear. Say something like: 'I agree with everything that's been said so far, but could I just add that we need to think about ...?'

Exchanging some information

Sometimes, you may want to give the benefit of your own experience or share new information. It's important to do two things: first, refer to the point you're sharing experience or information about; second, be concise. Once again the introduction is important. Say: 'Following up what Jan just said about the new working hours …', then go on to give your information. Do it like this: 'I've talked to a lot of my colleagues and their experience is …' or 'In my experience, people …'.

Disagreeing

The key here is to avoid causing offence. One way is to appear to agree first and then introduce the second magic word: *but*. Say: 'I agree up to a point, but …'. Sometimes, you can't avoid complete disagreement, but you can soften the blow by using phrases like: 'I'm afraid I have to disagree' or 'I'm sorry, I totally disagree.' Then explain why.

How to avoid making enemies

It's easy to make enemies in a meeting. Your style, what you say and the words you use can all irritate people. When you disagree, you go against other people's interests, and although you may be right, they may feel upset. Even if you disagree quite strongly in a meeting and say so, there are things you can do to help:

Separate the person from the problem.

Keep calm.

Put yourself in their shoes.

Make personal contact after the meeting.

If necessary, apologise.

If you are criticising a person's actions or opinions, always show you respect them.

Separate the person from the problem

This is the key piece of advice. People who are criticised in meetings often feel personally attacked. The trick is not to make the person feel offended, even if they are responsible for what you are criticising. People sometimes deliver criticism and then finish with, 'Nothing personal.' It might seem like a meaningless gesture but, delivered with a smile, it softens the impact of the heaviest criticism without diluting the message. When you disagree, always address the problem, not the person (even if the problem is the person). Depersonalise the argument: talk about 'It' or 'We', never 'I' or 'You'.

Keep calm

Even if you feel strongly about something, keep calm. Losing your temper or sounding het up makes a bad impression and can suggest you lack self-control. If you have a hot temper, cool it.

Put yourself in their shoes

Sometimes criticism may be for personal reasons which have nothing to do with the meeting. An example: Ian was irritable, and angrily criticised another participant. After the meeting we learned Ian's partner was in hospital. The participant he had offended told Ian she was sorry to hear the news. Ian was charming and apologised for his remarks.

Make personal contact after the meeting

Ian's story shows the value of personal contact after a meeting. If there has been a disagreement, explain to the person after the meeting why you disagreed. Always express the positive side first. Say: 'I thought you made some very interesting points but …'. In a one-to-one situation, you can explain your disagreement in more personal terms: 'I thought it was important to consider …'. Once again, this helps to introduce a more personal dimension, which is not always possible in the main meeting.

Sometimes, a personal chat is not possible; perhaps you don't have regular contact with the person concerned. In this case, make a phone call or send an email. When drafting an email, be positive. Start: 'It was good to see you at today's meeting. I really appreciated your contributions, but I felt …'. What you're really saying is: 'We may disagree, but it shouldn't affect our personal relationship as colleagues.'

If necessary, apologise

Never be afraid to apologise in the interests of maintaining good relations. Simply saying, 'I'm sorry if I offended you. I didn't mean to …' can improve the situation immensely.

How to follow up a meeting

This is very important. Someone in a meeting may reveal some information, mention a new contact or raise a new business opportunity. This is an opportunity to develop a new contact and show interest. Email straight away so you can get more information. Use phrases like: 'I was really interested to hear about ... if you could send me a copy, I'd really appreciate it.' Don't go into too much detail: summarise the information you're interested in, say what you want and thank the person. You may need to give your contact details.

It's very important not to ask for any favours at this stage, such as: 'Could I come and talk to you about it?' This is counter-productive. People are busy and don't have time. Any approach to ask for help or support will almost certainly be a turnoff. However, the person you have contacted may add at the end of their reply: 'If you need any more information, don't hesitate to come back to me.' If you want to, that's when you follow up. You might send a follow-up email: 'Sorry to bother you again, but could I ask your advice on ...?' Until then, ration your demands.

Sounding pro on the opposite page includes useful phrases and expressions. As you progress, you will learn expressions to use in meetings that express your personal style. To begin with, use these. They are polite and appropriate, and they will always show you in the right light.

Say 'Thank you'

If you enjoyed or valued what someone did or said in a meeting, you may want to thank them and say how useful it was. A short email to thank someone and to say you found it useful is gracious and will earn 'brownie points'. If you ask for someone to send you more information or a reference, always acknowledge and say thank you. It's a way of showing you've received the communication and closes off the exchange.

Sounding pro

Introducing yourself	Hello, my name's Jenny. I'm a publicity executive in Sales and Marketing. I'm responsible for promotions and I'm working with Ahmed, Head of Publicity.
Asking about minutes	Excuse me, what shall I minute?
Asking for repetition	Sorry, I didn't catch that. Could you say it again, please?
Asking for clarification	Could you clarify what you mean by that, please? / Could I ask you to explain in more detail?
Interrupting	Could I just come in here? / Could I just interrupt?
Asking questions	Could I ask if you have considered the impact this will have?
Adding a point	Can I just add something?
Offering information or experience	Following up what Mike just said about the new working hours … / Referring to the point about … / You may be interested to know … / In my experience …
Disagreeing politely	I agree up to a point, but …
Disagreeing strongly	I'm afraid I completely disagree. / I'm sorry I have to disagree with you.
Explaining your disagreement	I thought you made some very interesting points, but …
Apologising for causing offence	I didn't mean to upset you. / I'd like to apologise in case I caused you any offence.

Key take-aways

Think about the things you will take away from Step 3 and how you will implement them.

Topic	Take-away	Implementation
How to listen actively	• *Focus on the speaker's body language and feelings as well as their words.*	• *Don't interrupt.* • *Listen and observe posture, facial expressions and gestures.*
How to introduce yourself		
How to check information		
How to ask for clarification		
How to present an agenda item		
How to contribute to a discussion		
How to interrupt		
How to ask a question		
How to add a new point		
How to disagree		
How to avoid making enemies		
How to follow up a meeting		

Step 4

HOST VIRTUAL MEETINGS

'Silence is golden, except in conference calls.'

Five ways to succeed

- Make the intended outcome of the call clear.
- Talk to key players before the call.
- Check the facilities before you start.
- Check you are presenting the right company image.
- Make sure participants contribute if they wish to.

Five ways to fail

- Book the facilities at too short notice.
- Assume everyone will be online on time.
- Don't control who speaks when.
- Ignore issues affecting clarity.
- Assume everyone is happy to be treated the same.

What is a virtual meeting?

In a virtual meeting, none of the participants are physically present in the same place. They are all present on machines somewhere around the globe, so they are all together in one virtual space.

One reason why virtual meetings are so popular is because of restrictions on travel. There are three reasons for this: recession, security, and, most important, time away from the desk. As the world globalises, teams are increasingly spread over different countries.

At present, there are two alternatives for virtual meetings. One is communicating via telephone where you can hear but not see people; the other is communicating via video where you can see and hear people. Communicating via telephone is usually called a conference call and communicating via video is called video-conferencing.

Other technologies will doubtlessly come on stream and be used in business over the next few years.

In this step, we'll explore the advantages and disadvantages of each and show how you as a participant or meeting leader can get the most out of each type of meeting.

Via telephone

A conference call takes place via telephone or via a computer. People join from anywhere in the world. All they need is a phone number and an access code. Joining a conference call is simple: the meeting invitation (usually via email) gives you the number and access code. Simply dial the number (often a freephone number) and key in your access code. You may then be asked to say your name. When you've said it, you'll be 'admitted' to the conference call and away you go. Although the number that you ring is a freephone number, often the person/organisation organising the call will pay a monthly/annual fee for use of the number.

The conference call is an increasingly common way of getting people to talk to each other, and it joins executives together from all over the world.

Via video

A typical video-conference call room has a large TV (perhaps wall-mounted) on which you can see the other person or team, and a video camera which allows them to see you. You will need to use the remote control to set the video-conference up and if it's your first time doing this, it's good to have someone from IT on call to help you.

In most video-conference environments, the camera is fixed and can only see the whole group, but some cameras are now voice-activated and will zoom in to identify the person who is speaking. The most sophisticated is the *telepresence* room, which has dedicated seating areas and state-of-the-art recording equipment to ensure maximum quality of sound and vision. We'll talk about this and online meetings later.

Variations in technology

The exciting thing is that video-conference technology is developing all the time. It's important, however, to take into account that different teams may have access to different levels of technology. For example, if you see seven people uncomfortably hunched up together on a screen it may be because of a fixed camera. Everyone has to sit close together to be seen. Sound quality may be affected by the fact that there's a single microphone that's too far away to pick up quiet voices clearly.

Even on phone conference calls it can be difficult to hear people clearly. There may be voice distortion on the phone line or people may sit too far away from, or too close to, the telephone mouthpiece to be clearly heard. A lot of people complain that without the support of seeing facial expressions and lip movement, it's difficult to understand regional accents.

Where people are referring to information on computer screens, it's important to check that everyone has access to the same information. Information available to one participant may not be available to another for reasons of technology or confidentiality. Also, it's worth bearing in mind that there's usually a slight delay as the next screen or slide loads at the other end.

At the beginning of any virtual meeting, and especially when it's a first meeting, the meeting leader should check that everyone can hear and be heard clearly and that if they are sharing information from a remote source, that the same information is accessible to all.

The speaking skill

With remote meetings like conference calls, being clearly understood is very important. Four tips will help you be more clearly understood in a conference call:

■ **A-r-t-i-c-u-l-a-t-e**

You sound clearer and speak more slowly if you don't mumble. By opening your mouth and saying words clearly you'll immediately become easier to understand.

■ **Pause**

Many people speak too fast. As a result, it's hard to keep up. Pause very briefly before names, numbers, dates, places and events, and also between key sentences. 'Chunking' your speech like this will really help you to be understood.

■ **Explain acronyms and initials**

When you use an acronym for the first time, say what it is in full. You only need to do it once.

■ **Keep it short and simple (KISS)**

Say one thought per sentence and keep your sentences to between 15 and 25 words. This takes practice. Do two things: observe what you say. Then, if you observe that you're changing your mind, hesitating, or changing direction in mid-sentence, stop, pause and start a new sentence. You'll be much clearer.

If you are new to virtual meetings, don't try to do all four of these at once. To begin with, choose one and practise it. Then choose another, and so on.

Successful virtual meetings

Imagine this scenario. The head of HR in a leading London law firm manages HR for employees in other offices in Europe and she liaises with the HR managers in these offices, while her head of training and development is based in Australia. The head of HR, the European HR managers and the head of training and development meet twice a year at the conference in London, but travel is strictly limited. The head of HR's primary contact with the team is by regular conference call. They talk on the phone weekly. So, what are the ingredients for achieving a successful conference call?

■ **Time:** International participants are in different time zones. Even in the UK, participants may be available at different times. It's important to agree the timetable for the meeting in advance. A useful website is www.timeanddate.com, where you can type in the cities of the participants involved in the meeting and find suitable times in office hours for you to meet.

■ **Hierarchy:** Find out in advance who is the most important person in the group. Although in the UK the culture of informality rules, it may be best to address the most important person first and with special formality and respect.

■ **Clarity:** The limitation of a conference call is that people can only hear each other. This means clarity of expression is crucial.

■ **Technology:** As we saw earlier, check the level of technology of each meeting participant. Do they all have mute buttons? Do they all have access to the same information? In video-conferences, is the camera roving (i.e. able to zoom in on speakers) or static (i.e. fixed position)?

■ **Expectations:** In one-to-one or small-group conversations, find out in advance what people's expectations are – what they need to achieve from the meeting or key issues they need to discuss. Knowing participants' expectations can make a big difference between a successful conference call and an unsuccessful one.

■ **Size:** When it comes to conference calls, small meetings are better than big ones. Think about having a conference call with only a few people at a time. This may help quieter participants and non-native speakers of English. You can then delegate someone to summarise the discussion in the big meeting.

■ **Explaining the context:** Explaining the context is important in any meeting because people will feel more integrated into a strategy if they understand it, even if they don't completely agree with it. It's even more important for a conference call, because, at a distance, everything needs to be even clearer.

■ **Alternative communication channels:** For people who won't speak in public, ask them their opinion in private. They may find it easier to communicate their opinions in writing before or after the call.

■ **Sensitivity:** Being sensitive to different personalities is always important. At a distance, this awareness is even more important. If someone is shy, make sure they have space to speak. If someone dominates the conversation, they can be asked to be succinct and brief.

■ **Checking to avoid misunderstandings:** It's important to make sure that the right messages are communicated and that no misunderstandings occur. At a distance, misunderstanding can multiply. Useful techniques on how to run a meeting are discussed in Step 7.

Before the conference call

Check your equipment

If you're running a meeting, do a dry run. If you haven't run a conference call on the system you'll be using before, it's important to check the system works. Make sure you have an engineer close by or at the end of a phone in case there are problems with connectivity or sound. The key problems are likely to be sound dropout or complete failure to communicate with particular participants.

Lobby

By definition, you won't see the participants before the meeting, so if you're the meeting leader it's a good idea to contact everyone personally, or at least the key people, to tell them what you want to achieve and find out what their objectives are. It's a good way to get people on your side. And even if they disagree, you'll know where they stand.

During the conference call

The order of business is the same as for a regular meeting, but there are a number of things the meeting leader must pay attention to, given the fact that the meeting is virtual and not face-to-face.

1 Have the emails and numbers of all the participants to hand
People are often late, forget or have difficulty manipulating the equipment in conference calls. So it's a good idea to have their contact details to hand in case you need to locate them.

2 Have your mobile or laptop handy
Your main phone is being used for the conference call, so you need to have an additional resource for chasing up latecomers and no-shows.

3 Check equipment being used
Participants may be accessing the call from a variety of sources: landlines, mobile phones or computers. This may cause sound dropouts, distortions and variations in volume. It's as well to be aware of what might cause these. At the beginning of the call, check who's on a computer or handheld device. This may help if you need to give advice on how to improve reception.

4 Check sound
Make sure everyone can hear you and you can hear them. The best time to do this is in the introductory period when you check who is on the call.

5 Don't take equality and informality for granted
Different companies have different approaches to formality. So it may be a good idea to ask people how they would like to be addressed.

6 Welcome everybody

There's a standard way of doing this: 'Thanks for joining (the call). Let's just check who's here.' This is also a good moment to check on points 3, 4 and 5, but be careful not to extend the welcome. Extended introductions are one of a conference call's biggest time-wasters. A few minutes is more than enough.

7 Do a 'check-in' or 'check-out'

Some conference call meeting leaders begin with a 'check-in' or 'check-out'. This is a short period where people can ask questions and discuss issues outside the business. This might include events, questions about sports or celebrations, or maybe simply personal announcements. Meeting leaders claim it creates a good atmosphere, especially when conference call participants don't know each other. It serves the purpose of creating a positive team atmosphere.

8 Check silent contributors

In a conference call where you can't see people, it's extremely important to be aware of 'silent' participants. Be aware, however, that lines can go dead and people may just lose contact because of a poor telephone line. If any participants have gone silent, it's a good idea to check if everyone is still there. Say: 'Are we all here?' Others will quickly identify if someone has gone offline for no reason.

9 Always identify yourself

Remember, no one can see you, so when you intervene, identify yourself to the rest of the meeting. Say something like: 'Barry speaking. I think ...' or 'Barry here. I think ...', so people know who the intervention is coming from.

Virtual meeting etiquette

There are a number of problems specifically identified with virtual meetings. Here are some of the most common.

Open microphone

Some equipment is really sophisticated, with onscreen identification of speakers and mute buttons to silence your microphone when you're not speaking, but most equipment doesn't have these functions, so be careful of the following:

- Jewellery – are you wearing jewellery that rattles?

- Finger tapping – are you tapping your fingers? It sounds like thunder to everyone else.

- Pen clicking – you're listening, ready to take notes. Are you clicking your pen on and off so everyone else can hear you?

- Keyboard tapping – you may be taking notes or checking your emails. Once again, remember: everyone can hear your keyboard.

- Eating and drinking – these noises echo down the line.

Dead air

The ether is silent. Is anybody there? People may have been cut off or the line may be bad. However, it could be that some people won't intervene if their manager is on the call. That's the reason for identifying the manager(s) at the beginning of the call. In this situation, always address your questions to the manager first and let him/her nominate the respondent.

Background noise

It's a fact that with more and more people working from home, background noise is quite common. Traffic noise, children, doors slamming, all contribute to background noise. Echoey rooms may also create sound distortion. If you're participating in a virtual meeting from home, tell people you're on a call and for how long, so they won't interrupt you. Then choose a quiet room and close the door!

Heavy breathing

Some people naturally breathe quite heavily; maybe they have a cold or asthma. Whatever the cause, the effect is the same: distortion on the call. The call emphasises the noise. If you're a heavy breather, and people notice, it might be better to withdraw, if possible. Otherwise, try to sit back from the microphone when you're not speaking. If you're the meeting leader, and someone withdraws from the call for this reason, make a point of calling them afterwards to update them on results.

There's usually a mute button on the equipment that you can use while others are speaking. Don't forget to turn the mute off when you want to speak!

Limitations of technology

Video-conferencing

A video-conference call has several advantages over a phone conference call. The obvious, and most important, is that participants can see each other. One company noted that whenever a new project started, if the kick-off meeting included either a 'check-in' or 'check-out' session, relationships were notably warmer and easier to establish than in phone conference calls. Why? Simply because participants could see each other. People register body language quite as much as the words they use, and very often more. If they can see what people look like, whether they're smiling or frowning or how they dress, they often feel much better about each other and, as a result, find it easier to communicate. This is why it's often a good idea to use video-conference facilities for 'kick-off' meetings.

Video-conferencing is most effective across different sites within the same organisation. Organising video-conferences between different organisations is more difficult and it's easier to do this via an online link.

The problems are mainly harmonising the technology between the organisations and also checking participants have the same technical and physical access facilities. Video-conference rooms are often heavily in demand, so book up early.

Online meetings

This is useful technology for one-to-one or one-to-many communication. There are various options on offer, such as Skype™ or Skype group calls, and Google hangout. To participate, you need a webcam with a microphone. Lots of devices and laptops have these pre-installed already, so it's pretty straightforward. A problem is that picture resolution is not very high and faces can easily appear distorted. And have you noticed how people tend to look at the screen, not the camera? This means that, to the audience, they often appear to be looking away. To improve your screen image, don't sit too close to the screen and look at the camera, not at your own image!

Video-conference room

This is a dedicated room with a large screen for viewing the people you're talking to and a camera and microphone for recording. There's often a problem when there's only one camera and one microphone and the position of each is fixed. This means the field of vision is fixed and you can only get so many people within the camera's, and therefore the audience's, field of vision. This is why in video-conferences people often have to sit uncomfortably close together so they can all be seen. Technology is improving with voice-activated moveable cameras which 'zoom in' on the speaker, but not every organisation has this. One more problem: medium-sized and large companies never have enough rooms fitted for video-conferencing, and booking a room, especially at short notice, can be difficult. If you have limited technical facilities, limit the number of participants and make sure you plan ahead whenever possible.

Telepresence room

This is state-of-the-art: a specially designed table in front of a moveable voice-activated camera. A group of people sit in fixed position chairs facing a screen. When one participant speaks, the camera immediately recognises the voice and zooms in on the speaker. Afterwards it zooms back and focuses on the group, waiting for the next voice.

These are comfortable and well-furnished rooms but they have two disadvantages: the first is that you can have fewer people than the chairs provided, but you can't have more. So numbers are limited. Secondly, interrupting and rapid fire debate are discouraged. The camera can recognise, zoom in and zoom out, but it can't cope with interruptions and short remarks. So the system lends itself to disciplined and reasoned debate, not to argument.

This means that the meeting leader needs to select the participants carefully and control the meeting to make sure that every contribution is recognised. This also means stopping off-mic interruptions and comments and making sure that every comment is included on camera.

The future

Video-conferencing technology is evolving rapidly and it's exciting. It's certain that video-conferencing will increasingly take the place of phone conferencing and that there will be more facilities for individual participation from any location, perhaps using smartphone technology like *Google glasses*. These are interactive glasses which allow wearers to browse the Internet and also receive and send emails and talk, using their glasses as the screen. Nevertheless, for now and the foreseeable future there are a number of operational problems for meeting leaders and participants to consider.

Virtual meetings via video

In a virtual meeting via video, people can see each other. Not only that, they can see the room you're in and the table you're working at, and will judge how you look. What impression are you making? Here are six pieces of advice on making a good impression in virtual meetings via video. This is particularly important if the meeting is with external people.

■ What's on the wall?

Check the wall of the room where the video-conference is taking place. Is there anything inappropriate or revealing that outsiders shouldn't see? One company had a sales graph behind them on the wall showing plummeting sales figures. Another had compromising staff photos! A third had in view a confidential private phone number of a prominent member of a leading family. Check the wall. Does it promote your company? Is there anything compromising or confidential? If so, remove it.

■ What's behind the chairs?

When people are seated, are there things 'growing out' of them that can be seen on camera? Potted plants or advertising material are common problems. Has Jane got a potted plant growing out of her head? Has Jon got the ears of a bunny rabbit in an advertising poster coming out of his? Is an embarrassing slogan just above the head of the managing director, saying something like: 'Have you had yours yet?' Check the room, check the position of the chairs and remove or re-position anything you think might be compromising. Do another final check just before the meeting starts.

■ What's on the table?

Is the table tidy? Are papers organised or just strewn about? Are there empty coffee cups, sweet wrappers or half-eaten sandwiches on the table? Check and remove any mess before you start. An untidy table suggests a disorganised company.

■ How are you dressed?

Bright clothes are fine. But be careful of stripes – they strobe, creating lines on the screen. Are you dressed respectably? Does your dress code match the conventions of the other people? This may particularly apply if you're dressed too casually or reveal more flesh than is appropriate.

■ Can we see you?

Don't hide behind a large person next to you. If you are on the edge, don't lean backwards – you'll be out of shot.

■ Wave!

Six people on a video-conference can be hard to distinguish. When you start to speak, make a gesture or wave so everyone knows who's speaking.

Sounding pro: Post-meeting follow-up

If there is a technical problem or a sound problem during the virtual meeting, people may not be able to express their opinions. If this is the case, it's a good idea to follow up with an email after the meeting.

When writing a follow-up email, remember:

- Make sure your email is brief and to the point: keep to a maximum of five bullet points.

- Always start with positive points. Leave negative points till later.

- Always have a positive conclusion (advice or recommendations for action).

Dear Katie,

Following on from this morning's meeting, I would like to make these points about the proposal.

- *I like the idea of holding our meetings later in the day. I think it's a good way to wind up the day and prepare for the next.*

- *However, we must make sure that we don't cut out people who have to leave early. Many staff have to collect children from school and they get in early to make up the hours. If we hold the meeting too late, they will be left out of the loop.*

In conclusion, I think we should hold daily meetings at 3.30 or 4.00 p.m. and keep them short.

Regards,
Angela

Sounding pro

As you progress, you will learn expressions to use in virtual meetings that express your personal style. To begin with, use these. They are polite and appropriate and they will always show you in the correct light.

Welcoming and checking who's online	*Hello. Thanks for joining. Let's just check who's on the line.*
Letting others know you're online	*I'm here. Hi everybody, good to talk to you.*
Checking sound	*Can everybody hear me OK?*
Checking time	*Is everybody OK for a one-hour call?*
Asking people to adjust volume	*Could you speak up, please? / Could you get a bit closer to the mouthpiece?*
Checking sound quality adjusted	*Is that better? / Can you hear me OK now?*
Directing questions	*Clare, let me ask you first ...*
Intervening	*Alex speaking. Can I just make a point about ...?*
Dealing with heavy breathing	*Can you mute your microphone, please?*
Dealing with extraneous noise	*There's a clicking noise. Could you check it's not from your end, please?*
Explaining difficulties on the line	*It's a bad line. / I can't hear very well. / There's a lot of distortion.*
Checking on silent participants	*Are you all here? / Ahmed, are you still there?*
Checking the senior person in the other team	*Who's the team leader on this call? / Who's the senior person?*
Thanking the group	*Nice to talk to everybody, thank you.*

Key take-aways

Think about the things you will take away from Step 4 and how you will implement them.

Topic	Take-away	Implementation
How to identify and handle variations in conference call technology	• Recognise the different media and their advantages and disadvantages.	• Check each participant's technology at the beginning of the call.
How to improve your clarity of speech in conference calls		
How to manage conference call expectations		
How to prepare a conference call		
How to run a conference call		
How to identify and deal with conference call problems		
How to manage video-conference technologies		
How to prepare for a video-conference call		
How to run a video-conference call		
How to express your opinion in writing after a virtual meeting		

Step 5

USE INFORMAL MEETINGS WISELY

'There is no such thing as an informal meeting.
Every meeting enhances or diminishes
your influence.'

Five ways to succeed

- Make sure you know your point of view.
- Predict the point of view of the person you're meeting.
- Check your appearance and behaviour.
- Focus on the issue, not the individual.
- Be prepared.

Five ways to fail

- Assume it's 'just a chat'.
- Think it's not important.
- Get emotional.
- Ignore meetings rules.
- Assume there will be no formal outcome.

Informal vs formal meetings

Informal meetings are one-to-one or small group meetings which take place at short notice, in informal surroundings and sometimes out of office hours. There is no formal agenda (but there is always an agenda), no formal procedure and no record of agreement reached. However, a follow-up email is often useful.

Informal meetings take place in offices, in the canteen, in corridors and sometimes outside the office. They almost never take place in meeting rooms. They're often used to canvass opinion, test the water, lobby support or give or request personal advice, and the conversations themselves may be considered 'off the record' or confidential.

Many executives say that informal meetings are where the real work gets done. In many organisations they are where the real decisions get taken, which are then ratified and carried forward in the more formal meetings we have discussed so far.

Although informal in nature, these kinds of meetings have their own structure and protocol. If you learn the structure and observe the protocol, you will increase your influence in any organisation you work for, far faster and far more effectively than in formal meetings. So when a colleague or manager suggests a 'quiet chat', take it seriously. The results may be much more important and far-reaching than the occasion suggests.

Types of informal meeting

There are several types of informal meeting. The essential point to remember is that whatever type of meeting it is, and although it may be informal, its outcomes may influence your work, your prospects and your record. The message is this: even if it's informal, always be prepared.

Canvass opinion

Meetings where people canvass opinion are one-to-one or small group meetings aimed at finding out what individuals think about an issue or topic. They may be telephone conversations or face-to-face meetings, but they are informal and serve to prepare the ground for the formal meeting later on. The trick here is to try and maintain a balance. Show you understand all sides of the debate: 'On balance, I think …'.

Test the water

An example: Jane wanted to apply for a new job in a different department of the organisation she worked in. First she spoke to her manager and arranged an informal meeting. Her manager suggested she should email the department head to introduce herself and explain her interest in the job. Then Jane and the department head had an informal chat in the canteen. Jane was encouraged to apply for the job formally and she ended up getting a new job from a process which started as an informal meeting.

Lobby support

Lobbying occurs when a proposal is already on the agenda and its supporters try unofficially to persuade other members of the group to support it too.

Ask for and give advice

Learning how a new organisation works is never easy. There are all kinds of procedures and protocols, both official and unofficial, and you can only learn them as you come across them.

That's why it's important to know when and how to ask for advice, especially when it comes to the red tape, i.e. office rules.

■ **How to ask for advice** First, be clear about the advice you need. It's difficult for someone to give advice if you haven't identified the problem for them. Maybe the problem is simple. Say something like: 'Excuse me, I don't understand all the paperwork we have to complete for the new ordering system.' Try to make sure the answer isn't something you can easily find out for yourself. Say something like: 'Excuse me. Can I ask your advice?' Then explain what the problem is.

CEO coffee

In some smaller organisations, the CEO invites a department or a group of selected employees to an informal meeting, not in the boardroom or his/her office but in the canteen or relaxation area. The aim is to create a more relaxed atmosphere.

How you behave in this environment is important. It's a great opportunity to meet the CEO personally, learn how he/she thinks and to register yourself with him/her. Listen carefully and take the opportunity to ask constructive questions or make positive suggestions when the opportunity arises. It's your opportunity to get noticed, but remember three key things: listen carefully; be positive at all times; and make only constructive suggestions.

Check-in

Normally you 'check in' and 'check out' when you arrive at or leave a hotel. In this context, 'check-in' and 'check-out' refer to an informal period when people can ask questions about anything they want outside the scope of the meeting. This may be five or ten minutes at the beginning or end of a meeting. It's very popular when people don't know each other very well or on conference calls where they haven't met personally. It allows time for people to get to know each other and exchange information about their personal and social environments.

■ **What do you talk about?** Obviously, you don't want to get too personal, but it's always interesting to know where people are from, how they joined the company, and their personal interests, including travel and holidays. This can lead to interesting discussions.

Just a quiet word ...

This is the moment when someone calls you aside to give you informal advice or feedback, warn you about something or tell you about something you've done wrong. The person will do it in private so as not to embarrass you. Maybe you will have to do it as well, to a colleague. How do you do it diplomatically, and what's the right reaction? What can work well is the 'observation, feelings, needs' model.

Imagine Jane has been getting in late for work. A colleague or manager notices it and calls her aside for a quiet word. The conversation might go like this.

Manager: (*observation*) Jane, I've noticed you've been getting in late this week. Is anything wrong?

Jane: No. It's just that my alarm clock is dodgy. I've been getting up a bit late and I've missed my usual bus.

Manager: (*feelings*) Well, your work's very good and usually you're on time. It would be a pity if getting in late got you a bad reputation.

Jane: But it's only this week. And I've been working late to make up for it.

Manager: (*needs*) I know, but Jim's a stickler for punctuality. Try and get in on time from now on. Make a point of it. OK?

■ **Positive first** Did you notice how when the manager was expressing her feelings about Jane's lateness she started off by saying, 'Your work's very good.' If you're going to make a recommendation to improve behaviour, always try and find something positive to say first.

Drop-in meetings

Sometimes, you need to set up your own informal meeting, and it may be necessary to interrupt your manager or colleagues. This is a 'drop-in' meeting.

You could drop in to their office or go to their desk and check when would be a good time to meet. But be careful: they might be busy. Check before you interrupt. Is the person on a call, with someone else or about to leave for another meeting? Some people discourage drop-in meetings and won't allow them unless they're in the diary. If the person you want to speak to has an office and the door is closed, they're probably unavailable. If it's open, it's probably OK to put your head round the door. In open plan offices, you'll need to use your common sense.

If you do drop in, make it quick. Say: 'Sorry to interrupt, but can I just ask a quick question?'

Show your sensitivity to other people's time.

Alternatively, if they look busy or are about to go into another meeting, you could interrupt them to set up a time for a future informal meeting. You could say: 'I'm not sure how busy you are today, but I'd like to discuss something with you. When would be good for you?' Again, being sensitive to your colleague's time and availability will mean that you get a better result. They will choose a time that suits them and then they will give you the time you need.

If you're asking someone who you work with frequently or get on with, a simple enquiry is sufficient: 'Are you free for a minute?' or 'Have you got a minute?' If your colleague is busy, simply say: 'Can you let me know when you're free?' and that will do the job.

Receiving feedback in an informal meeting

It's always helpful to receive informal feedback. In a formal context, it's an essential part of reviewing performance and consists of telling people what they did well (positive feedback) and what they could improve (negative feedback). The term *negative feedback* is seen as demotivating, and managers often prefer to talk about 'challenges' and 'opportunities for improvement'.

Feedback operates at two levels: performance (what you did well and not so well) and attitude (how you behave towards colleagues, clients and management). People will give feedback on both. Most managers prefer to say something positive first. For example, you may hear, 'We're very pleased with your work here so far, but …'. Be careful. The important message is what comes after the 'but': '… but we try to keep a clean desk policy here and yours is currently the untidiest desk in the office.'

■ **How to take feedback** It's easy to say, but difficult to do. First of all, try not to take negative feedback personally. See it as a learning opportunity. As an employee, you need respect, recognition and appreciation. Negative feedback may feel like a denial of all three, but in fact it's an opportunity to earn them. Whether you earn them or not depends on how you respond. Simply saying, 'That's useful feedback, thank you' earns respect. If, after you've received feedback, you're unsure how to proceed, you might say: 'My problem is that I don't have much space. What would you recommend that I do?' The resulting advice will resolve the situation and, as long as you follow it up, it will earn you brownie points.

Strategies for responding to informal feedback

As we've said, receiving negative feedback can be uncomfortable. But there are other strategies you can use to manage the process satisfactorily. Here are five pieces of useful advice.

■ **Focus on the facts** Ask questions to identify the real interests at play. In the clean desk scenario, Jon could have asked: 'I'm sorry, could you tell me what the policy is?'

■ **Keep it polite** This is really important, especially if you're receiving advice from a manager or senior colleague. Remember the time-honoured British style of asking permission to ask a question. Beginning a question with, 'Could I ask you ...?' or 'Do you mind if I ask you ...?' can defuse any kind of aggression on the part of the person giving feedback.

■ **Don't take it personally** Remember, this is performance improvement not character assassination. Depersonalise the criticism if it's negative and, if you receive praise, be pleased but don't get too puffed up.

■ **Stand up for yourself** If you feel you're being unfairly criticised, be prepared to say what you do well. Be prepared to say: 'I don't think that's fair.' But once again, focus on the facts.

■ **Small improvements get big results** People aren't usually looking for radical changes in behaviour. Normally, they are looking for small changes to show you have taken the feedback on board and are heading in the right direction. Small incremental changes are what get long-term results.

Informal meetings: preparation

Unofficial meetings are, by nature, impromptu, so you may not have much time to prepare. However, you always have time to collect your thoughts. One reason informal meetings can be a shock is because people don't prepare themselves properly. Remember the Scout motto: 'Be prepared.'

■ **Think: What do you want?** Ask yourself: Why am I attending this meeting? What do I want to get out of it? What do I need to say?

■ **Think: What does the other person want?** In your own mind, review why the other person wants the meeting. You may be wrong, but it's better to go into a meeting with an idea of what you expect than with nothing at all.

■ **Come as you are** In an informal meeting, there's no time to plan your outfit. If you have time, you could nip into the rest room to make sure you look presentable.

■ **Get into listening mode** Whatever your expectations, you may be surprised. Tell yourself before you go that you're in 'listening mode'. Listen and don't react until you know clearly what the situation is.

■ **Grab your notebook/tablet** If you're at your desk when someone asks you for a 'quiet word', grab your notebook or tablet and head off.

In the meeting

Whether it's five minutes or longer, there are certain strategies you need to adopt when you're in the meeting. As you get used to informal meetings, things will become automatic, but initially you may have to remind yourself.

- **Keep your powder dry** This was advice given to soldiers in the nineteenth century before automatic rifles were invented: if your gunpowder is wet, the gun won't fire. It means you should save your resources until you need them. Listen quietly, attentively and appreciatively.

- **Ask questions** Having listened, ask questions to clarify your understanding of the situation and what's needed. Use phrases like: 'If I understand correctly …'.

- **Don't get emotional** Don't overreact if someone says something that upsets you. In business, a level-headed approach is appreciated.

- **Check action needed** There are two types of check here. The first is what action to take. It's entirely appropriate to ask: 'What do you want me to do?' The second is to double-check what's expected of you. Once again, questions like: 'Can I clarify. You want me to …?' are fine here.

- **Check follow-up** Always make sure that if you have additional questions, you can go back to the other person and follow up. Ask questions like: 'Can I call/email you if I have any other questions?' Normally, the other person will say it's fine.

The follow-up

After the meeting, there may be certain things you need to decide and certain actions you need to take. Your decisions here will help determine your reputation for efficiency, organisation and reliability.

Do I need a record?

The problem with verbal conversations and short informal meetings is that people can forget what they agreed. So it's worth checking: would a short email confirmation be worthwhile? A 'paper trail' to record what was agreed, even in informal meetings, may be worthwhile. This is especially true if the informal meeting involves details, in particular numerical details, that could be miscommunicated. You'll see this from Jon's email on the next page. If anything goes wrong, you have a record of what was discussed and agreed. It doesn't need to be formal, but note that best practice is to copy the style you receive. If in doubt, however, always be a bit more formal.

Note that it's not always necessary to send a follow-up email or action anything. Sometimes an informal meeting is used to get your opinion on something that is off the record. In this case, no follow-up is needed. It very much depends on what was discussed at the meeting as to whether or not you decide to follow up with an email.

Remember that if someone sends you something, it's polite to acknowledge it with a simple email saying 'Thank you', 'Thanks', or even 'thks'.

Sounding pro: Follow-up email to check action agreed

To: Marlene   From: Jon
Re: Meeting

Hi Marlene,

Just to confirm, you wanted me to check invoice 14513 against deliveries and confirm product QVOA 1515 has been received by our Manchester office, in order to authorise payment. I'll phone them and get back to you to ASAP.

Thank you.
Jon

Keep people up to date: As discussed on the previous page, it may be a good idea to follow up on the agreed action. If you are going to do this, do it quickly. The next thing to think about is keeping people up to date on progress, especially on delays. You need to demonstrate that you're proactive. A quick phone call or email will suffice. In Jon's email, he rang the Manchester office and found that receipt of the product hadn't been entered in the deliveries log. However, staff thought they had received the product and it was in the warehouse. They said they'd check and call back. Jon emailed Marlene to tell her, so it was on the record. Jon was doing his job and being proactive.

To: Marlene   From: Jon
Re: QVOA 1515

Hi Marlene,

I phoned and checked QVOA 1515. Manchester confirmed it is not entered in the delivery log. But they think it's in the warehouse. They will call back. I'll keep checking.

Thanks.
Jon

How to give informal advice

Up to now, it's been all about taking advice and feedback, but a colleague may ask you for your advice. How do you give it?

- **No blame, no shame** First of all, show respect for the person asking. Sometimes people might ask for advice on how to deal with a mistake they've made or to recover from an embarrassing situation. Never comment on the person's behaviour.

- **Think about the problem not the person** Focus on the problem. Get it clear before you give any advice.

- **Don't impose a solution** Avoid 'should' and 'must'. Be objective. Say: 'This happened in the Birmingham office and what they did was …'. Alternatively, say what you would do, as in 'If I were you, I'd …'.

- **Offer positive options** If you can't help, always try and suggest someone who can. People will respect you much better for it.

Getting the style right

There's informal and there's very informal. Informal meetings are, by definition, more relaxed than formal ones. But there are a few 'no-no's' that you should keep in mind. Monitor your own communication style. Do any of these apply to you?

- **Greetings** Avoid the 'Wassup?' ('What's up?') style of greeting. Be relaxed and agreeable but not over-casual. Remember there's casual and there's smart casual.

- **Dress code** Observe the office dress code. Is it formal or smart casual? Even 'dress-down Fridays' have their own protocol. 'Casual' is just another dress code.

- **Ration the slang** People may be insulted, think it is inappropriate, may not understand it or, even worse, take it seriously.

- **Take it easy on the jokes** Senses of humour differ. Constant banter may result in people not taking you seriously. Sarcastic humour hurts and may make enemies needlessly. Charm, not humour, often wins the day.

- **Avoid code** If you use acronyms and initials, don't forget that not everyone will understand them. Be prepared to spell out acronyms and initials when you use them the first time.

- **Beware of discrimination** It is illegal to make derogatory remarks about religion, race, gender, age, disability and sexual orientation. Watch your tongue – and your 'off the cuff' remarks.

Recovering from a 'car crash' meeting

The meeting went wrong. As far as you're concerned, you created no rapport, achieved no recognition and deserved no respect. Is there anything you can do? Yes, so let's look at the symptoms and solutions.

■ You lost the plot

Symptoms: You talked too much, you went off the point and introduced irrelevant subjects. You probably felt insecure, so you needed to make your presence felt.

Solution: Hold your tongue. If you do that, the other person will value what you say much more. Remember: the best talkers are listeners.

■ You disagreed – loudly

Symptoms: You talked loudly, you seemed to be in permanent disagreement with the other person. He/she probably thought you were inconsiderate and insensitive.

Solution: Speak more quietly, and if people look at you, ask yourself: 'Am I too loud?'

■ You were always on the defensive

Symptoms: Someone commented on your behaviour or attitude, even slightly negatively, and you were instantly on the defensive, or you attacked back.

Solution: Listen carefully. If the point is broadly accurate, you'll gain more respect if you admit to it than if you defend yourself against it. Remember: the apparently negative comment you feel most defensive about may be true.

■ You were stubborn

Symptoms: You refused to accept anyone else's suggestions or modify your position in any way.

Solution: Say you are open to suggestions and ideas and will consider them. Never reject out of hand, even if you can't accept them.

■ You tried to dominate the meeting

Symptoms: You hogged the meeting. You talked too much. You got emotional. You even told the group how important you are, or used to be in another environment. It was insecurity once again. You needed to feel recognised.

Solution: Don't focus on yourself. Listen to other people and when someone makes a good point, recognise it and endorse it. That will get you the positive recognition you crave.

■ You used sarcasm too much and too often

Symptoms: You constantly made fun of people, made sarcastic comments and damned with faint praise. Others may have laughed at the time, but ultimately you came across as a negative influence, and they were scared of your sharp tongue, so tried to ignore you.

Solution: Curb your tongue. Use your wit and observation to show appreciation of people. This way, your occasional sarcasm will be seen as wit and humour, not, as may appear now, bitterness.

■ You provided too much, or too little, data

Symptoms: You rolled out huge amounts of facts and figures. No one knew where they came from and no one cared. Alternatively, you produced no facts and no data. It all sounded like hearsay and received opinion. People ignored what you had to say.

Solution: Select your information. Two 'killer' facts, and sources to support your argument, are better than too many or none at all.

■ You tried to be funny

Symptoms: You couldn't resist a joke or a clever or flip remark. You wanted to display your huge sense of humour or show how sharp and clever you are. Unfortunately, it had the opposite effect. The others assumed you were a 'smartass' or 'too clever for your own good' or, even worse, 'not taking the matter seriously'.

Solution: Check before opening your mouth. Keep your sense of humour under control unless you know it has a place.

Informal meetings audit – assess your performance

We all have to attend lots of meetings. As we have seen, informal communication is an important part of our work. It's worth reviewing our own participation in, and attitude to, informal meetings in order to assess how we can improve. Here are six questions we can ask.

1 Is my participation level strong?

1 Not really involved ☐ 2 So so ☐ 3 Variable ☐ 4 Generally strong ☐

Take the attitude that there is always something to learn. You'll be more positive.

2 Am I a good listener?

1 More of a talker ☐ 2 So so ☐ 3 Variable ☐ 4 Generally good ☐

Do you talk too much?

3 Am I open to feedback and suggestions?

1 No ☐ 2 So so ☐ 3 Variable ☐ 4 Generally yes ☐

Do you consider other people's suggestions before responding?

4 Do I deviate and go off the point?

1 More of a talker ☐ 2 So so ☐ 3 Variable ☐ 4 Generally good ☐

If you lose the plot, notice it. Stop talking.

5 Do I try to dominate meetings?

1 Whenever I can ☐ 2 Often ☐ 3 Occasionally ☐ 4 Never ☐

Listen to others. Don't interrupt.

6 Do I make my points in a clear and measured way?

1 No, I rely more on emotion. ☐ 2 So so ☐ 3 Variable ☐ 4 Yes ☐

Keep the balance. Remember your two 'killer' facts.

Add up the numbers to get your total score. If you scored 23 or less, review the information in Step 5.

Sounding pro

As you progress, you'll learn expressions to use in informal meetings that express your personal style. To begin with, use these. They're polite and appropriate, and they'll always show you in the correct light.

Checking understanding	If I've understood correctly, what you'd like me to do is …
Clarifying information and decisions	Can I just clarify …? / Can I just check …?
Checking access to further information	Can I call you if I have any further questions?
Checking someone's availability	Sorry to bother you, but have you got a minute? / Sorry to interrupt, but can I just ask a quick question?
Responding to feedback	Thank you. That's good advice. / That's useful feedback. / What would you recommend that I do?
Asking questions politely	Could I ask you …? / Do you mind if I ask you …?
Checking your understanding	Let me check. If I understand correctly … / Can I clarify, you want me to … / What do you want me to do?
Asking for advice	Excuse me. Can I ask your advice? I've got a problem with …
Giving advice: avoiding *should* and *must*	If were you, I'd talk to my HR manager. / Maybe it would help if you …
Responding to negative feedback	What would you recommend that I do?

Key take-aways

Think about the things you will take away from Step 5 and how you will implement them.

Topic	Take-away	Implementation
How to prepare for informal meetings	• *Recognise the factors in an informal meeting.*	• *Think what you want. Think what the other person might want.*
How to behave in an informal meeting		
How to follow up an informal meeting		
How to avoid being too informal		
How to ask for advice		
How to give advice		
How to give feedback		
How to receive feedback		
How to recover after making a bad impression		
How to assess my performance in informal meetings		

ADAPT TO MEETING DYNAMICS

'Getting good players is easy. Getting 'em to work together is the hard part.'
— Casey Stengel (1890–1975), Major League baseball player

Five ways to succeed

- Communicate your key objectives clearly and consistently.
- Know when to dominate, facilitate and listen.
- Encourage everyone to contribute.
- Deal with difficult and unexpected situations decisively.
- Finish on time.

Five ways to fail

- Assume the meeting can run by itself.
- Let other participants take over the meeting.
- Allow the discussion to ramble on.
- Stop expression of ideas.
- Don't minute action points.

Meeting styles

To get the most out of a meeting, ideally the meeting needs an effective meeting leader. This doesn't always happen, however, and sometimes a strong participant ends up taking over. Here we talk about the dynamics of a meeting, so you can observe what's going on in meetings and learn from your experiences.

The three meeting leader styles

There are three kinds of meeting leaders: *the dominator, the facilitator*, and *the follower*. Each has some advantages and disadvantages. We all have a bit of each one at different times.

- **The dominator:** The dominator gets things done, runs the meeting firmly and does most of the talking. He/she gets results.

- **The facilitator:** The facilitator gets things done too but, in a less interventionist way. He/she structures the meeting and guides the process along. He/she is also sensitive to participants' needs and encourages silent participants to contribute.

- **The follower:** The follower focuses on structuring the meeting but lets others lead the discussion. This allows a strong personality to dominate the meeting.

The good leader

The three styles are not exclusive. The good leader is probably a combination of all three styles and maybe uses one or another at different stages of the meeting. The dominator takes decisions, the follower listens and absorbs information. The facilitator encourages and nurtures each participant.

The advantages and disadvantages of each style

Dominator, facilitator and follower may correspond to different personal styles, but they're also roles. A good meeting leader knows instinctively when each role is necessary, sometimes adopting all three in one meeting.

■ **Dominator:** The dominator gets results, but at a price. Other participants may feel angry and resentful. It can also mean that important but quieter voices don't get heard. The dominator role occurs when the meeting is going nowhere and needs to be driven forward to get a result, maybe because two members of the meeting can't agree.

■ **Facilitator:** The facilitator checks time and reminds participants to keep to the agenda. He/she also watches how participants are feeling. A good facilitator constantly reads the room. Who is yawning? Who looks distracted? Who is leafing through documents? Who looks bored? The facilitator should ask questions or invite contributions to draw people out, so participants feel much more motivated. This is a really important role, but it has two downsides. The first is that important issues may not get the space they need for proper discussion. The second is that less gets done or, if there is too much discussion, outcomes are less clear. The facilitator role occurs when there are participants who are silent and it's important to hear their views. They need to contribute, and need space and time to speak in the meeting.

The facilitator also focuses on ensuring the participants respect the three Ts: *time, topic* and *temperament* (we'll discuss these later).

■ **Follower:** Followers defer to expertise and experience within the group. This approach works when there is an acknowledged expert who is in a position to lead a particular point in the discussion. The follower gives respect to the expert view and makes sure he/she has time to share his/her experience. But the follower role can be a disadvantage if one or two strong-voiced participants take over the meeting. At worst, the meeting leader loses control of the meeting. In some cases, the wrong decisions may be made just to suit a strong personality's ego.

Moderating one's role

In acknowledging the strengths and challenges of each role, it's important to appreciate the role your personality plays. Some people are naturally firm and decisive. Others are natural facilitators, some are happy as followers, as in the cartoon below. Self-awareness is the key. Recognise your style and be prepared to adapt to the situation, as necessary.

Assess the dynamics

When you're in a meeting, observe the meeting leader and ask these questions:

1 Is the meeting leader too dominant? Are other participants getting a look in?

2 Does the meeting leader feel that the only views that matter are his/hers? Is the meeting leader listening to the others?

3 Is the meeting being dominated by one or two voices?

4 Is the meeting leader failing to impose his/her authority and risking losing control?

5 Is the meeting leader deferring to an expert who clearly has more knowledge and experience? Is there a danger of the expert taking over the meeting?

6 Is there too much discussion and inadequate focus on action points or clearly identifiable outcomes?

7 Is the meeting running smoothly and to time?

8 Is the meeting leader encouraging quieter people to participate?

Now check:

■ If the answer to questions 1 and 2 is *Yes*, the meeting leader is likely to be a dominator.

■ If the answer to questions 3–6 is *Yes*, the meeting leader is likely to be a follower.

■ If the answer to questions 7–8 is *Yes*, the meeting leader is likely to be a facilitator.

After a meeting, review what worked and what *didn't* work. What were the times when things went wrong? Remember what you learned for when you have to run a meeting.

The three Ts – time, topic, temperament

The three things a meeting leader needs to control in order to maintain control of a meeting are *time, topic* and *temperament*. Observe these.

Time

Meetings need to start and finish on time. If they don't, people get exhausted and impatient, and the decisions are often made in haste just to get people out of the meeting. In other words, they are often short term. They may not be the right solutions for the long term. Also, have you noticed that if a meeting is due to finish at 11, your brain tends to turn off or turn to other things at about 10.45? A good meeting leader will aim to finish on time or, if the topic is important, renegotiate the timetable.

If you need to renegotiate the timetable, make it clear, get agreement and don't over-extend the new deadline. A common way of doing this is to ask: 'Can we spend another 15 minutes on this? Does anyone have to leave at the scheduled time? … Thanks. So we'll aim to finish at 12.45 sharp.'

Another time problem is people talking too much and taking too long to make their point. Once again, it's the meeting leader's job to control this. They might say: 'We're running out of time. Could you sum up briefly, please?' The key word here is *briefly*.

If the meeting leader can't complete the agenda in time, it's important to prioritise. 'We won't complete the agenda at this meeting. Can I suggest we cover items 4 and 7 and postpone the others till the next meeting?'

Topic

It's easy in a meeting to go off-topic and start talking about your own concerns. Once again, it's the meeting leader's job to keep the topic on track. One of the best ways to do this is to refer to the agenda, and say something like: 'Can we keep to the agenda?'

Temperament

We all want to make our point in meetings and sometimes we can express our views quite passionately. Meeting participants might get quite confrontational when there are strong feelings on either side of an issue. Displays of temperament are not helpful and in many countries, especially Asia, they indicate lack of self-control and unreliability. So in a meeting where someone gets a bit over-emotional, attacks a colleague or even the meeting leader, how does the meeting leader contain the outburst? He/she should politely tell people to calm down and suggest discussing the issue later on, outside the meeting.

Observations

We've explored the styles of dominator, facilitator and follower. We've also explained how each style may be necessary in different meetings or even at different times in the same meeting. Now we'll look at what skills are needed to run a good meeting.

Starting the meeting

It matters how the meeting leader starts the meeting. How he/she looks, the tone of voice, being positive or serious, and making a confident opening all contribute to the success of the meeting. Failure in these means the rest of the meeting may be spent trying to reverse that first bad impression. Phrases like: 'Thanks for coming'; 'We've got a lot to get through today, but I'm sure we'll have a positive outcome'; 'What I want to achieve today is …' all help to establish a positive and dynamic image.

Guiding the meeting

A meeting leader is responsible for reminding participants of the key objectives of the meeting and ensuring smooth progress through the agenda. At the start of the main part of the agenda, the meeting leader should remind participants what he/she expects to achieve and highlight the key agenda issues, if any: 'Let me just remind you that we need to decide on …' and 'The key issues we need to address at this point are …' are useful 'reminder phrases'.

Keeping to time

Very important, this. The meeting leader should monitor the discussion, ensuring each item is brought to a close in good time and not let participants run on. If necessary, the meeting leader should be prepared to interrupt and ask people to conclude. Appealing to the shortage of time is a good idea: 'Sorry, to interrupt. We're short of time. Could you sum up, please?'

Summarising key action points

It's important to ensure that at each stage of the meeting a clear decision is reached before moving on. Once again, the meeting leader should be prepared to take the lead and summarise the discussion: 'Let me sum up …'; 'We agree that …'.

Checking the minutes are taken

The meeting leader needs to ensure that the minute-taker minutes each decision, using the *what, who* and *when* process (see Step 2). He/she may also want to record one or two observations by participants, if relevant: 'Let's minute that the meeting has approved the increase in budget. Sean will be responsible for it and will report on progress at the next meeting. Let's also note that Freya expressed reservations about the increase in budget at this stage.'

Avoiding or dealing with disagreement effectively

Watch how the meeting leader finds ways to deal with strong disagreement or conflict, either by agreeing a decision or dealing with disagreement in a separate meeting. Phrases such as: 'We'll just have to agree to differ' or 'Let's discuss this outside the meeting' are appropriate here.

Dealing with unscheduled events

People arrive late and leave early. There are changes to the agenda running order and sometimes other problems. How does the meeting leader cope? Simply, juggle the agenda items or even move them to the next meeting. But they should never lose sight of their key objective.

Transitions

It's important to be able to move between agenda points smoothly. When preparing the agenda, the meeting leader creates a story with a smooth progression from one point to the next. It's important to close off one point and then move on to the next. Some meeting leaders simply say firmly: 'Item five. Sheila, will you introduce that?' Others may have a longer transition: 'So that deals with item four. Let's go on to item five.' Making sure the progression is properly signalled is an important part of running a smooth meeting.

How to summarise a discussion

This can sometimes be challenging: the meeting is running on, a lot of arguments are presented, and they need to be brought together and summarised. Occasionally, a meeting participant will do this. Usually, however, it's down to the meeting leader. What can he/she do? First, ask three questions:

What is the conclusion?

How does it relate to the meeting objectives?

What are the next steps? (The next step becomes the action point.)

Let's take an example: the decision to change working hours. How do we manage that? Some participants want flexible working hours to allow parents with young children to leave early. Some want fixed working hours because they believe it's the easiest way to control the payment for part-time workers. Others want to introduce a degree of working from home to reduce pressure on office workspace. Still others oppose it – they believe that too much working from home will reduce productivity and affect team spirit.

How does the meeting leader summarise this? What are the next steps? How does he/she know what to minute as an action point?

There are two issues: flexible hours vs fixed hours and home working vs office working.

What are the next steps? Probably, to survey staff wishes to get objective data to base a decision on.

Who should do it? The HR manager.

By when? A month – report at the next meeting.

And that's the action point: *HR manager to survey staff needs and report in one month. The decision is to get more data.*

115

Assess and clarify what is agreed

As we've seen, participants may have very different views on the agenda item under discussion. It's important to assess who agrees with whom and make sure they have all agreed the same thing. There is only one way to do this: summarise the debate in your own words, reformulate the arguments and check that the participants agree.

Summarising a discussion involves a number of processes. First, you can summarise who thinks what in your own words: 'Let me summarise the discussion as I see it.' Then you can summarise the main arguments: 'As I understand it, Jack, you believe that …, but Anna, you think that …'. Secondly, you can give your own opinion: 'In my view, what we need to do is …'. Finally, when you've achieved agreement, simply summarise the action point.

Confirm what has been agreed and minute accurately

After an intense discussion, it's easy to forget the minutes. It's important to be clear about what has been agreed and to minute that accurately. If no agreement is possible, the decision may be to discuss the issue 'outside the meeting' or to 'raise the issue at the next meeting'. That gives you time to lobby participants and try to reach an agreement.

In some cases, there is continuing disagreement. The aim is to find the majority opinion. However, be prepared for the fact that some participants may continue to disagree and wish to file a minority opinion. This must be noted in the minutes.

How to control a meeting

How does the meeting leader maintain control, especially in a difficult meeting where there are strong personalities and strong feelings? There are two areas of control that are important: control of the meeting procedure and control of the discussion. In meetings that you attend, take the opportunity to watch what's going on. Does the meeting leader maintain control?

Controlling the procedure

Think of these five rules:

Keep to the agenda.

Control the discussion.

Start and finish on time.

Sum up the discussion.

Agree on action points.

Controlling the discussion

Think of these five rules:

Facilitate the discussion.

Make sure everyone is involved.

Don't just stay with what you expect. Encourage different views.

Decide what needs longer and what needs shorter discussion.

Recognise creative contributions and good ideas.

The seven stages of control

What needs to happen to maintain control effectively throughout the meeting? Here are seven key stages for the meeting leader:

Stage 1: Take charge immediately

Call the meeting to order firmly, introduce participants and move through the first part of the agenda quickly and efficiently. Be polite and considerate to all participants.

Stage 2: Introduce each agenda item

Introduce each agenda item and ask the appropriate participant to discuss it. If necessary, summarise their contribution briefly.

Stage 3: Open and manage the discussion

Invite contributions from the group. Manage the contributions using the *tough and tender tactics* described on the next page.

Stage 4: Agree what to minute

For each item, agree what to minute and advise the minute-taker.

Stage 5: Conclusion

Towards the end of the agenda, it's often useful to summarise the most important action points.

Stage 6: AOB and date of next meeting

It's important to move efficiently through AOB so that it doesn't extend beyond the time allocated for the meeting. Announcements should be brief and to the point. The standard phrase is to announce: 'AOB. Let's go round the table.' Propose the date of the next meeting.

Stage 7: Thank everyone and close the meeting

A good meeting leader interposes his/her authority at each stage of the meeting, from greeting participants to closing the meeting. Failure to do this means the meeting could be taken over by stronger participants.

Dealing with talkative participants

Some meeting participants seem to love the sound of their own voice. Others don't know how to speak concisely and go round and round as if trying to find the point they want to make. Still others consider themselves important because of their status, experience, prestige or expertise. People like this in meetings can be intimidating to deal with. How should the meeting leader deal with them? They need to move things on, but they also need to avoid antagonising the participant in question. There are two strategies – the tender tactic and the tough tactic.

The tender tactic: interrupt, thank, continue

The meeting leader should first interrupt and stop them speaking. Then thank the participant and maybe compliment them: 'Excuse me… thank you. That was very helpful.' Then simply say: 'Can we move on?' or some other phrase to close that contribution.

The tough tactic: interrupt, stop, continue

The meeting leader should use this tactic when the participant doesn't want to stop and insists on continuing. In this case, the interruption needs to be polite but very firm: 'Sorry, I have to interrupt you here.' Then they need to stop the contribution continuing: 'We've got the point' or 'You've had your say.' Then continue: 'Let's move on.'

Only use tough tactics if absolutely necessary. Courtesy, politeness and consideration for all participants are very important in successful meeting leadership. Remember, the meeting leader's job is to 'deliver' the meeting successfully. That's where their authority lies. They shouldn't let anyone compromise it.

Encouraging quiet participants to contribute

Creating an open atmosphere where everyone feels they can contribute freely is an important meeting leader skill. They need to make sure everybody's voice is heard. If they do this, everyone is reasonably happy. If they don't, they risk some people being frustrated, resentful and uncooperative. However, some participants prefer not to be called on. How does the meeting leader handle them? The meeting leader should:

■ Do his/her homework

This means finding out what they can about each participant's areas of experience and expertise *before* the meeting. That way they can identify potential contributors to the discussion.

■ Establish a principle of openness

By their attitude and in what they say, the meeting leader should make it perfectly clear that they are open to discussion on the item under consideration: 'I'm open to any ideas' or 'Please feel free to intervene on this point.'

■ Look for contribution signals

People often signal that they would like to contribute. They may open their mouth, make a hand gesture, nod their head or even just lean forward. The meeting leader should look out for these signals and check if they mean the participant in question wants to contribute.

■ Control interventions

Sometimes a participant opens his/her mouth to speak and another participant jumps in. The meeting leader only has two options – one is to stop them: 'Sorry, Dan. Nina intervened first. Nina, go ahead.' The other is to allow Dan to speak, but to go back to Nina immediately afterwards: 'Nina, you wanted to say something.'

Dealing with difficult situations

There are a number of difficult situations that can arise in meetings, regarding both facilities and participants. What's the best way to cope with them? First, let's look at the types of problem and where we can expect them to arise. We'll also suggest tactics for dealing with them.

Facilities

Double-booking of rooms, room too hot or too cold, room too small, PowerPoint facilities not working – these can negatively impact a meeting. The answer to these problems is improvisation. The meeting leader needs to stay calm. Some of the participants in the meeting may help to find a solution. It may involve changing rooms or doing without PowerPoint. Most people will adapt if the meeting leader does three things:

- recognise the concern
- explore options
- agree on the best course of action.

This may involve having a shorter meeting in an unsuitable room and putting off all but the major decisions till the next meeting. The meeting leader needs to be flexible.

Sticking with your plans despite poor facilities may be counterproductive. Participants may be in a bad mood, uncooperative and unwilling to engage in discussion. They may just want to leave. If you have to stay in poor facilities, do what you can to make it more comfortable and make sure everyone has time to get a coffee or tea before you start.

Participants

When dealing with difficult participants, there are both strategic and tactical things the meeting leader (and the other participants in the meeting) can do. There are four key strategies:

■ Treat people as they are, not as you would like them to be.

■ Deal with people as they are now, not as they were in the past.

■ Treat people as individuals.

■ Take a risk. Trust people to do the right thing.

Impatient people These are the people who want a decision now, even without discussion. They can't see why you waste time discussing things when the decision is obvious! The meeting leader should intervene to get them to be patient: 'I appreciate your wish to get a result, but we need to hear other viewpoints first.'

Know-it-alls These participants don't understand why others don't accept their views. They need to be blocked politely: 'Thank you for your view. I think there are other views we should hear before we reach a conclusion.'

Duellists These participants don't like each other much or are very competitive. No matter what the topic, they will always disagree with each other or undermine each other. Stop the duel: 'You've both got valuable points to make, but we need to preserve a balance. Can we hear from someone else?

Phone users These are the participants who can't tear themselves away from their smartphones and tablets and spend most of the time checking emails and messages. Ask a personal question to refocus their attention: 'Fred, what do you think of Amy's suggestion?'

Sounding pro on the opposite page includes some of the key phrases a meeting leader needs to maintain control of a meeting and run it smoothly.

Sounding pro

As you observe meetings, note down other phrases that seem useful, so you can devise your own 'meetings phrasebook'.

Starting the meeting and establishing objectives	Thank you all for coming. / What I want to achieve today is … / Let me just remind you of our key objectives…
Keeping to time and topic	Sorry, we're running out of time. Could you sum up briefly, please? / Can we keep to the agenda, please?
Avoiding or dealing with disagreement	Let's agree to differ on this. / Let's discuss this in a separate meeting.
Dealing with talkative participants	Excuse me. Thank you. That was very helpful. Can we move on? (*tender*) / Sorry, I have to interrupt you here. We take your point. Now let's hear from someone else. (*tough*)
Dealing with impatient people	I appreciate your wish to get a result, but we need to hear other viewpoints.
Encouraging quiet participants	Please feel free to intervene on this point. / Sorry, Dan. Nina, go ahead.
Summarising a discussion	Let me sum up the discussion. As I understand it, Alex, you believe that … but Elena, you think that …
Dealing with unscheduled events	Let's deal with this point at the end of the agenda. / Let's raise this issue at the next meeting.

Key take-aways

Think about the things you will take away from Step 6 and how you will implement them.

Topic	Take-away	Implementation
The different types of meeting leader styles to help meetings run more smoothly	• *Dominator — when the meeting is going nowhere and needs to be driven forward.* • *Facilitator …* • *Follower …*	• *Note at which point of the meeting each type is needed.*
How to deal with issues around time, topic and temperament		
How to identify the skills of the meeting leader		
How to summarise discussions		
How to control a meeting		
How to deal with talkative participants		
How to encourage quiet participants		
How to deal with difficult situations		

Step 7

RUN EFFICIENT, EFFECTIVE MEETINGS

'Management is about arranging and telling. Leadership is about nurturing and enhancing.' — Tom Peters, international management guru

Five ways to succeed

Know your objectives.

Keep to time.

Achieve the goals of the meeting.

Motivate the participants.

■ Make sure everyone knows what they need to do.

Five ways to fail

Be vague and unclear in communicating objectives.

Overrun time.

Allow or create unnecessary discord.

Have no clear follow-up on action points agreed.

Have no contingency plan for non-completion.

You are unlikely to be running meetings in the very early stages of your career, but it's good to learn about it early on so you can observe others and carry it out effectively when asked.

A successful meeting starts before anyone enters the room. The person running the meeting, and every participant, needs to have clear objectives. Why? Because every meeting needs to have a purpose. If it doesn't have a purpose, it's unlikely to have a result.

To achieve your objectives, decide:

what you want to achieve

how to achieve it

who to invite (see Step 1)

what type of meeting

how to structure the meeting.

To structure your meeting, think of these things:

the problems you need to address (agenda items)

the likely answers (action points)

who is responsible (action point owners)

when you need results (deadlines).

Your objectives will vary according to the type of meeting, but, as discussed previously, will usually fall into one of four categories:

Exchange of information

This covers updates on projects and operations, identifying possible delays, and troubleshooting problems. These are routine meetings which take place every week or month, depending on the company. They normally take the form of reports from each person on their area of responsibility, followed by discussion.

Survey of opinions

Sometimes a meeting is held just to find out people's opinions on a topic. This might be a single issue or a series of issues. With this type of meeting, sometimes no decision is taken at the meeting. The opinions expressed during the meeting provide the basis of the decision, whether it's made in the meeting or later on. This kind of meeting will normally result in a commonly held view or series of views which will make it easier to take a decision.

Action to be taken

Most meetings in the UK result in an action plan. This is a clear decision leading to action. We call this the *what, who, when* process. *What:* this is the action point. What the organisation will do as a result of the discussion. *Who:* this is the action point owner. We sometimes say *process owner*. The owner is the person responsible for making sure the action point is carried out. *When:* this is the deadline. When should the action point be completed? Often the deadline is ongoing. In this case, the *when* may simply be 'update on progress at the next meeting'.

Responsibilities to be taken

This is a meeting to allocate jobs – to decide who will do what. This meeting may be part of the action planning meeting or it may be a separate meeting on its own, especially if a lot of people are involved. This kind of meeting is often used to reorganise workloads or restructure departmental responsibilities in response to changes in the organisation's needs.

The basics of running a meeting

In Step 2, we discussed the two types of meeting – the regular meeting and the 'one-off' meeting, and the agenda for each. If the agenda is the spine of the meeting, the steps of the agenda are the vertebrae, the small bones that make up the spine. The individual agenda times are the ribs. The one-off meeting will have a few less vertebrae than the regular meeting and only one or two ribs – a strange animal. However, it will broadly follow the shape and style of the regular meeting.

Here is the order of business for a relatively formal regular business meeting. In a 'one-off' meeting there is no previous meeting, so no minutes received, matters arising or sign-off.

The pre-meeting

The pre-meeting is what you do before dealing with today's agenda. Here are the stages, slightly more detailed this time:

1 Call to order
2 Welcome and greet participants
3 Apologies for absence
4 Nominate someone to take the minutes
5 Check any agenda changes
6 Check minutes received and matters arising
7 Sign the minutes
8 Today's agenda

Let's walk through each one and find out what happens.

1 Call to order

This is the official start to the meeting. In a very formal session, the meeting leader may say: 'Let me call the meeting to order.' Most meeting leaders are less formal: 'Right, let's kick off', is a much more common beginning.

2 Welcome and greet participants

Thank everyone for coming. Check everyone knows each other by 'going round the table' and asking everyone to introduce themselves in turn. Speak up, be clear. All you need to say is your name and what department you belong to or what organisation you represent. For example: 'Barry Tomalin, author, HarperCollins.' This helps everyone identify you and understand your area of responsibility.

3 Apologies for absence

We know what this is (see Step 2), but how do you do it? The formal way is to say something like this: 'We have apologies from …'. The informal way is something like: 'Hamid can't make it. He's on leave today.' It'll depend on who your meeting is with as to what you say.

4 Nominate someone to take the minutes

If you haven't pre-arranged this (though it's much better to do so), now is the time to nominate someone. The simplest way is the best: 'Sophie, could you take the minutes, please?' It's not a good idea to ask: 'Could somebody take the minutes?' It's much better to be specific.

5 Check any agenda changes

This is the time to propose any changes in the order of items for discussion. Some meeting leaders can be quite inflexible. In this situation, any new items for discussion may be added to the end of the agenda 'if there's time'.

6 Check minutes received and matters arising

This is a standard request: 'Did everyone get a copy of the minutes?' What follows is more interesting: 'Any matters arising?' This is the opportunity to suggest amendments to the minutes of the previous meeting. Perhaps a piece of information has been recorded wrongly and needs correcting. Perhaps an action point in the minutes, recorded as completed, is still outstanding. In this case, the meeting leader has three options: to make the amendment; to add the point to the current agenda; or to discuss it in a separate meeting. If it's to go in the current agenda you may hear: 'Let's raise this under item 5,' or 'Let's raise this under Any Other Business.'

7 Sign the minutes

This isn't very common, but in some large organisations and associations it's necessary to record that everyone agrees the minutes are a fair and accurate record of the meeting. This is in case there's a problem in the future and people need to refer back to the minutes to find out what happened. However, in some countries, signing the minutes is still the norm.

8 Today's agenda

Once the minutes from the last meeting are agreed and, if necessary, signed by the meeting leader, the meeting is ready for the current agenda. The meeting leader signals this very simply: 'Let's move on to today's agenda.'

Note that in a 'one-off' meeting, items 6 and 7 are ignored. Item 5 may also not be relevant if there is only one item for discussion.

Today's agenda

'Today's agenda' has four main areas. We'll deal with each in turn.

- Agenda items
- Final summing up
- AOB (Any Other Business)
- Date of next meeting

1 Agenda items

This is often the most difficult part of the meeting, where the different issues get discussed and sometimes argued over. However, it helps to remember that any single agenda item usually goes through three clear stages:

1 Report   2 Discussion   3 Conclusion

- **Report** At the report stage, the person responsible for the agenda item introduces the topic. They may already have submitted accompanying paperwork (as we discussed in Step 2), which participants should have read. However, they are busy people and often don't. That is why the wise person responsible for the agenda item will summarise the key points in a few sentences, 'just to remind you', before stating their own position. When they state their own position they will probably say three things. First, what has been done, second what the situation is now and finally what needs to be done next.

- **Discussion** At this point, the meeting leader opens the agenda point to discussion. Participants make their points and maybe argue over certain points. How the meeting leader keeps control of all this is something we discussed in Step 6. However, at some point the meeting leader will sum up. This is at the conclusion stage.

The important thing is to make sure comments are to the point and don't take longer than necessary. It's also important that everyone gets a chance to contribute if they wish to. Ensuring this is part of the meeting leader's job.

■ **Conclusion** The meeting leader concludes the discussion, sums up the action point and tells the minute-taker what to write. This needs to be simple, quick and, if possible, uncontroversial. Use the *what*, *who* and *when* process. For example, 'Let's minute for item 5 that we will send a follow-up letter to the company demanding action. Frank, you'll do this. And can you report back on progress at the next meeting?' Finally, signal that it's time to move on. Say: 'OK? Let's move on to the next item on the agenda.'

It's not always easy to end a lively or heated discussion. One of the marks of a good meeting leader is an ability to terminate a discussion without causing anger or resentment. A common approach to discussions that get too lively is to appeal to the clock and say: 'We're running out of time. Can we come to a conclusion?'

2 Final summing up

It's often a good idea to highlight the main action points at the end of the meeting before going on to Any Other Business. This allows people at the meeting to note the priority points to address after the meeting is over.

3 AOB (Any Other Business)

This is a mopping-up operation. It allows the meeting to deal with smaller, often bureaucratic, items that don't fit into the main business of the day. It also allows people to announce unexpected developments, for example, a recent sales success. As we said earlier, it's an opportunity to deal with items that weren't included in the main agenda but need brief discussion.

The important thing about AOB is that it should be brief. Go round the table one by one and ask if there is any other business. The participants either raise a point or say 'No'. If they raise a point, the meeting leader has to make three decisions. What to minute, whether to put the item on the agenda for another meeting to allow fuller discussion, or simply to let it pass. The key question is: might we need to refer to it in the future? If not, don't minute it.

4 Date of next meeting

The final act is to fix the date of the next meeting. Once again, the meeting leader should lead on this. He/she should suggest the date, time and place so the participants can check their diaries and agree.

A word about tradition

Some of this might seem quite formal and old-fashioned. Remember that meetings are part of an organisational procedure that has evolved over very many years and has worked successfully. However, the procedure is only an organisational tool. Even though the principles may be sound, the practice may be different in different industries and different organisations.

One of the key differences is style. The style can be quite formal or it can be informal. The style of the meeting leader is important to success. It's also important to adapt the meeting leader's style to the environment. Older managers, for example, can be very put off by what they see as an overly relaxed and, as they see it, careless approach to business.

In some organisations and professions, you may find the terminology very formal. 'Chairman' or 'Madam Chairman' might be used to address the meeting leader, and you may hear phrases like 'on a point of order' or 'on a point of information'.

Another key difference is environment. A meeting on a factory floor, in a hospital canteen or in a shopping area in a store may be different in style from a meeting in a boardroom, but the structure will be more or less the same.

A third difference is what's included. We have seen that in a one-off meeting the minutes of the last meeting and 'Matters arising' are redundant. However, in a more casual meeting other things may be left out, such as 'Apologies', 'Any Other Business' and 'Date of next meeting'.

The following are most important and should always be included: key agenda points; introduction; discussion; and noting *what* will happen, *who* will be responsible and *when* the action will be completed.

Sounding pro

Over time, you'll develop your own set of polite phrases to manage a regular meeting. Until then, here are a few suggestions. Observe how different meeting leaders run meetings, so you can learn from them.

The pre-meeting

Calling the meeting to order	Can I call the meeting to order? (*formal*) / Let's kick off. (*informal*)
Welcoming and greeting participants	Hi everyone. Thanks for joining the meeting. / Let's go round the table and introduce ourselves.
Apologies for absence	We have apologies from John. (*formal*) / John can't make it today, he's on leave. (*informal*)
Nominating someone to take minutes	Sally, could you take the minutes, please? / As we discussed, you're taking the minutes, Sally, thank you.
Checking any agenda changes	Any changes to the agenda? / Does anyone have anything to add to the agenda?
Checking the previous minutes and matters arising	Did everyone get the minutes of the last meeting? Any matters arising? / OK. Let's raise this under item 5.
Signing the minutes	Let's take the minutes as read.
Moving on to the main agenda	Let's move on to today's agenda.

Today's agenda

Introducing agenda items	Item 1: Carolyn, could you introduce this? / OK. Let's move on to the next item on the agenda. Item 2 …
Managing the discussion	**Encouraging contributions:**

Encouraging contributions:

Any contributions? / Leila, do you have anything to add?

Managing disagreements:

Let's agree to disagree. / Let's discuss it outside the meeting.

Managing digression:

Could you keep to the agenda, please?

Keeping to time:

We're running out of time. Can you come to a conclusion, please?

Deciding what to minute Let's minute for item 1 that we'll send a follow-up email demanding action. Fran, you'll do this. And can you report back on progress at the next meeting?

Concluding the agenda That concludes the agenda. The main action points to note are …

AOB Any other business? Let's go round the table.

Setting the date of the next meeting Let's fix the date of the next meeting. / The next meeting is on Tuesday week. OK?

Circulating of minutes Max, could you send me the minutes ASAP so I can check them before circulation?

Follow-up

The final part of a meeting is the follow-up – what happens after the meeting is over. This is where it can all go wrong. The effort of planning and organising, and the energy generated by the meeting can all be dissipated if there is no follow-up or if the follow-up is not prompt.

The follow-up stages

There are two stages in the follow-up process:

■ finalising the minutes

■ circulating the minutes.

Stage 1: Finalising the minutes

Don't lose time in getting down to this. The meeting leader needs to get together with the minute-taker as soon as possible after the meeting, and certainly no later than 24 hours, to go through and finalise the minutes. If a personal meeting isn't possible, then it's still important to exchange information by email and possibly follow up with a phone call. The aim is to ensure everything has been covered: that the *what*, *who* and *when* for each agenda item are clearly stated and there is nothing to embarrass or cause problems for the company or organisation.

Stage 2: Circulating the minutes

It's important to circulate the minutes as soon as possible. Leaving it for a few days or, in some cases, until just before the next meeting, is a really bad idea. It means there won't be enough time for action points to be followed up.

Chasing up the action points

You may think that following up action points is an automatic process. It's not true. When people get back to their desks, their routine takes over: there are emails to deal with, calls to return and other meetings to attend. The action points on the minutes sink to the bottom of the pile. So there is a third stage in the follow-up process, but whether you do this stage or not depends on your position in the organisation. If appropriate, you might be expected to chase people to action the points they are responsible for from the meeting.

The way to do this is to follow up with an email to the relevant person. How much you end up chasing your colleague will depend on the importance of the action point, the urgency of the deadline and the reliability of the person responsible for the action point.

Creating the virtuous circle

Action points in the minutes of a meeting are important as a recommendation for action, but the action won't happen by itself. It needs motivation and practical support. If the meeting leader can do this there are several practical results:

- First, people will see that the meeting is not just an academic exercise. There is a result and the result is real, not just a paper decision.

- Second, as a result, more people will come to meetings because the meeting leader has demonstrated the value.

- Third, more people will take the action points seriously and will initiate action without waiting to be pushed.

- Fourth and lastly, there will be an unexpected outcome. The creation of a virtuous circle.

A virtuous circle occurs where every component works well and each part reinforces the other: we attend the meeting; we note the action points; we follow up and we report to the next meeting on our progress. Hey presto! The virtuous circle is complete! The opposite, of course, is the vicious circle: we attend the meeting; we note the action points; there is no follow-up; we report a delay and we miss the next meeting. The sense of decisive action disappears. Cohesion and dynamism dissipate. The department, if this goes on, becomes a candidate for restructuring and amalgamation.

Obviously, the failure to complete minutes and follow up on action points are not the decisive factors in a failing process, but they are important contributing factors. And one of the first signs that something is wrong is late or incomplete reporting and follow-up.

The people side

So far, we've looked at the meeting as a way of deciding on a group of objectives to be achieved. This is done through the action points, but meetings are made up of people and people have needs too. These needs may have nothing to do with the action points or the meeting purpose. Looking after participants' personal needs and wants is also part of the meeting leader's job. The first task is to recognise them. Here are some non-action-point points to bear in mind.

The meeting leader

If you're the meeting leader: remember that administrative staff are also vitally important to the success of a meeting. 'Meeters and greeters', guides, reception staff and tea-makers all contribute to the good atmosphere of a meeting. It's important for you to recognise their contribution and thank them publicly. They will feel recognised and valued.

Imagine you're leading a meeting and someone is unhappy about something. What should you do? Ask the participant how they're feeling. Do this outside the meeting or perhaps during a break. You should do what you can to reassure the participant personally, while emphasising the needs of the organisation.

In the case of unhappy or disappointed participants, you may not be able to satisfy their complaints. In this case it is really important to explain the situation so that the participant understands the limitations of what is possible. You will probably find that they will accept the situation even if they are unhappy about it.

The participants

Whatever your role in the meeting, do it well. If it's preparing documents, booking rooms, taking minutes or even just making the tea, do it efficiently and with a smile. Someone will notice. They'll thank you. You will feel more part of the group and you'll feel better. Practical administrative tasks are part of making meetings work. Take pride in your part in helping the meeting succeed. Even if participants don't mention your role, they will still notice it. Even more so if you do it inefficiently or with bad grace. See Step 3 for more on how to be a good participant.

Conflict in meetings

Any meeting, any group, in fact, goes through four stages, especially when the participants come together as a new group. The four stages are:

■ forming ■ storming ■ norming ■ performing

This is recognised as an important general management concept and it especially applies to meetings.

Forming This is when the group gets together and they size each other up. It happens in every meeting. Watch and listen to how people greet each other. Listen to the small talk. Participants are trying to check what mood their colleagues are in. Will they be receptive to ideas?

Storming When the meeting gets into the agenda points, there may be a fair degree of disagreement about causes of problems and courses of action. This is the storming phase of any meeting – the discussion of difficult agenda points.

Norming At this stage, the meeting leader has resolved any disagreements on content or approach and the meeting can proceed in relative harmony. All meetings need to arrive at a *norming* stage in order to perform. A meeting which remains at the *storming* stage will achieve little, except continuing disagreement and frustration.

Performing This is the stage where the meeting can effectively move forward as one unit, discuss issues, agree decisions and follow them up efficiently. Performing is the action stage, the point at which it is agreed who will do what and by when.

Why failure to norm matters

The failure of a group to norm in a meeting is often a reason for the failure of meetings. One of the reasons for a failure to norm is that the individuals look at their own frustrations and interests rather than the business needs of the organisation. That's why having a positive attitude in meetings and looking for what will move the business forward is so important. Whether you are part of the meeting, part of the administration of the meeting, or simply an observer, your efficiency, willingness and good humour are essential contributions to the all-important norming process. In other words, you are more important than you may think.

How to control the process

In any meeting, storming and norming go on all the time. There is always agreement and disagreement on key points. The meeting leader's job is to keep the storming process under control and, if possible, friendly, and to move towards a performing point where decisions can be taken and acted upon.

How do you do this? First, by recognising what stage the meeting is at. Secondly, by always remaining detached from the discussion, no matter what the provocation or incentive might be. Thirdly, by ensuring that the meeting stays calm and insisting that any major disagreements be settled outside the meeting. Fourthly, by moving as smoothly as possible to the performing phase by ensuring agreement on action points in line with the key objectives.

Key take-aways

Think about the things you will take away from Step 7 and how you will implement them.

Topic	Take-away	Implementation
How to set clear objectives in meetings	• *Review key activities and identify key areas for action.*	• *Make sure your agenda covers your objectives.*
How to recognise and adapt to the different types of meeting		
How to use this to run meetings more smoothly		
How to deal with the pre-meeting		
What steps to go through to run a successful meeting		
How to minute action points		
How to follow up the meeting		
How to show awareness of people's needs		
How to recognise the different stages of a meeting		